June 2011 —

Charlotte it has
been a blessing!
work with you this
past year especially MSW!
you completed your MSW!

Love and blessings!
Shawn Harriott

Praise for *Pressing into Thin Spaces*

"Somehow we know that we were made for so much more than the things of this world. Nestle into a comfortable chair and follow Margaret to a thin place where the invisible realm comes into focus. Get ready to experience God and fresh revelations of hope."

—PAM VREDEVELT
Best-selling author of *The Power of Letting Go,*
The Wounded Woman, and *Empty Arms*

"How beautifully Margaret portrays the thin places—the tender places—the most significant places of our souls. Her work is compelling and rich with passion. It is gripping, challenging, deeply moving. The canvas she paints not only reveals a vulnerable woman, but the brilliance of a mighty Savior. Ever revealing, ever present, a loving God who sees the painful, yet breathtaking realities of our lives. A God who reveals Himself in life-giving color. A God who sees you. Struggling to find the thin places of your life? This book is the first thing I would put in your hands."

–TAMMY MALTBY
Cofounder of It's a Good Life
Media personality, TV cohost, and speaker
Author of *Confessions of a Good Christian Girl* and *The God Who Sees You*

"Margaret Wills' *Pressing into Thin Places* brought hope to my soul like the sight of crocuses pushing through the frozen snow-covered ground. Resurrection life is real and it often surprises us in the bleakest of winters, as these well-written stories reveal."

–DEE BRESTIN
Author of *The God of All Comfort* and *The Friendships of Women*

"Just as there are seasons of the year, there are seasons of life. There are happy times and there are times of darkness, discouragement, and despair. There are spring and summer seasons, and then there are, at times, very long winter seasons. One thing that's needed in every season, but especially in the difficult ones, is encouragement. The gift of encouragement brings light into darkness, renews hope, and provides perspective. Sometimes it's all that's left to keep someone from giving up . . . it's a gift Margaret is generously giving to all of us in the form of this book."

–Dr. Gary J. Oliver
Executive Director of the Center for Relationship Enrichment
John Brown University

"Wills' book touched my heart! The diverse themes with the ever-prevailing golden thread of God's consistent and unconditional love are the message we are pursuing when in need of encouragement. [Wills'] writing style makes the reader to want to read on! This is a book that you will go back to from time to time for words that resonate with your life challenge of the moment."

– Sister Judith Marie Keith
Religious Sister of Mercy, Fort Smith, Arkansas

"The poetry and prose of *Pressing into Thin Places* do not offer facile or simplistic answers. It is a book that does offer the power of the archetypal scriptural leap of faith in dealing with the losses and tragedies that everyone must face and even the everyday pettiness to which all succumb. I like what Margaret Wills has to say and how she says it!"

– Shirley Forbes Thomas
Retired Professor of English and Director of Honors
John Brown University

"I've been a fan of Margaret Wills' writings for more than 25 years. This book is a source of encouragement to anyone who needs strength, hope, or courage. It is scripture-based and helps us refocus our thinking. It is exactly what is needed for anyone who is ready to move forward in life."

–Rick Renner
Senior Pastor, Moscow Good News Church
Moscow, Russia

PRESSING INTO
THIN PLACES

PRESSING INTO
THIN PLACES

Encouraging the Heart
toward God

Margaret Harrell Wills, EdD

BCP

Pressing into Thin Places
Encouraging the Heart toward God

Brown Christian Press
A Division of Brown Books Publishing Group
16200 North Dallas Parkway, Suite 170
Dallas, Texas 75248
www.brownbooks.com
(972) 381-0009

Serving with Excellence.™

ISBN 978-1-934812-99-0
Library of Congress Control Number 2011922647

Printed in the United States.
10 9 8 7 6 5 4 3 2 1

For more information about Margaret Wills and *Pressing into Thin Places*,
please visit pressingintothinplaces.com.

A portion of the proceeds of the sales of *Pressing into Thin Places*
will go to John Brown University Center for Relationship Enrichment

This book is dedicated to Paul,
my longtime, beloved best friend,
and constant encourager.

Contents

IV. The Fall

V. Speaking in the Waves

VI. A Listening Heart

VII. Our Starting Place

VIII. The Way to Your Door

IX. The Reality of Living

X. Beauty from Ashes

XI. Rebirth

XII. Amen

Acknowledgments

Any creative work is, in some way, indebted to those who have had an impact on one's life. I have been influenced by many writers but much influenced by family and friends. Their hearts—large, loving, and generous—have given me a sweet taste of God's love.

To my sons, Alan and Shawn, who will know how much I love them when they look at their own children.

To my daughters, Patrice and Amy, who make me grateful and graft me into their love and life.

To my grandchildren, Caroline, Braden, Abigail, Mia, and Fisher, who never cease to charm me and warm my heart with their wit, wisdom, and joyful hearts.

To my sisters and brother, Shawn, Betsy, Jackie, and Bill, whose love is rooted in our heritage and our unceasing, unbounded friendship.

To my soul mate sisters, Suzie and Susan, who together are a ray of sunshine and a sheltering tree.

To Dr. Rex and Judy Russell, whose friendship reaches back and looks forward.

To my walking women, who listened and laughed while I walked by their sides.

Author's Note

When the challenges of life come, there is help and there is hope. The prophet Isaiah declares, "A bruised reed He will not break and a dimly burning wick He will not extinguish" (Isa. 42:3 NASB). People down through the ages have testified to the faithfulness of the Lord. He is trustworthy in every aspect of our daily living.

This book expresses the universal fears, trials, disappointments, and joys that we experience in our day-to-day journey and encourages the heart and mind toward God by pointing to the wisdom, hope, and faithfulness of the scriptures and the Holy Spirit.

This book encourages us to press into thin places in our spiritual life. As we follow Jesus and walk toward God and His Truth, there are times when we feel especially close to God, where for a moment the spiritual and the natural worlds intersect and narrow into a thin place, a place of sudden, momentary awareness of the deep presence of God. This is a book that recognizes the thin air of the mountain peak but realizes we live sometimes in the valley and often on the flatlands. It is a call to the application of faith in all areas of life and at all times.

We are created to connect with God and restore the relationship we innately and desperately desire. We are called to be followers of Jesus. This book encourages us to be honest in our need and expectant in our faith. It points us to move toward the heart of God and find the joy and reality of "God alive in us."

God is good and God loves us,
Margaret Harrell Wills, EdD

Introduction

There are two common myths that have taken unfortunate root in the hearts and minds of many Christians, and they are two of the most dangerous lies to believe. The first is that once you give your heart to Jesus Christ, your every problem will be solved and your life will be easy and pain-free. The second is its close kin—the belief that if trouble, hardship, or sorrow enters your life, then you must have fallen out of God's favor and wandered away from His plan for you.

While God does at times use discipline or tribulation to correct or guide, to believe these lies—that your life as a Christian should be a carefree romp through the daisies, and if it isn't, that God is no longer smiling down on you—is to risk overwhelming fear, discouragement, and a loss of the peace and joy that we are meant to have at all times, even times of trial.

The truth of the matter is that we live in a fallen world, a world of pain and heartache; even Christ and His disciples had to pass through storms. It is to this world and these storms that Margaret Wills writes, and it is to you and to me, making our way through the storm while the deck of the boat pitches beneath us and the cold waves threaten to take us under. Margaret reminds us that if we are safely in the boat with the Captain at the wheel, we can let go of our fear and trust the One who can still the waves with a word.

As many have said, we are not promised an uneventful journey, only a safe arrival. In the meantime, Margaret encourages us to press close to the source of our peace, to discover the "thin places" that allow us to glimpse another truth: that there is a world beyond this fallen one that our eyes can see. This world we can see is not our home, and Margaret's stories and poems remind us that there is always something working behind the curtain, beyond the veil. On the other side, a Father waits with open arms to welcome us back to where we belong.

This book is also about those times when the waves are still, the boat is drifting peacefully, and the sun is sparkling on the crystal waters. Margaret encourages us to join her in her wonder at the beautiful and mysterious workings of creation, to marvel at the awesome and heart-stopping complexity of this world of ours, with its creative design beyond our comprehension. We can cling to faith in times of trial, but we can also rest, praise, laugh, and worship.

Margaret writes of hopes, fears, dreams, grief, joy, and struggles that are at once intimate, personal windows into her life and also common human experiences that you and I can relate to in a place deep inside: the death of a parent, the faithfulness of a friend, the struggle to make a marriage work, the loss of a child, the desire to feel God's presence, the desperation to know His will, and the determination to learn from the past while making the most of the future, to name only a few.

These pieces will speak to people of all backgrounds, but Margaret's collection is more than a "how to cope" manual; it is a glimpse into the heart of the One who gives her reason to hope, hold on, and shout for joy. And here's the good news (and couldn't we all use some good news?)–that heart is patient, merciful, generous, and abundantly loving. If you have not yet been introduced to this God, this book is for you, and you will know Him better through these pages. If you already walk with Him, this book is for you, and you will find encouragement and comfort herein.

This world can be a disheartening place. One has only to turn on the news to experience this daily. It's easy to lose courage in the face of such unrelenting darkness, which is why we are meant to lift each other up and direct each other's gaze back to the light. It is why we are explicitly told: "In this world you will have trouble. But take heart! I have overcome the world" (Jn 16:33 NIV). Amen.

–Tim Boswell
October 2010

I

THIN PLACES

Aaron

Oswald Chambers in his book, *Christian Disciplines,* says that the "unexplained things in life are more than the explained." I recall the time I flew to Phoenix to be present for the birth of my sister's first child. Betsy is my baby sister, fourteen years younger than I am. I mothered her from the moment she was born. She was the flower girl in my wedding and she made me promise to step on every petal she threw on the floor. I was there as Betsy gave birth to her first child, a severely brain-damaged son, a son named Aaron. A baby was born. I grieved at the stillborn joy.

I recall standing in the hospital hall, peering into the nursery with my head and hands helplessly pressed against the glass. I remember back at her room standing at the head of her bed with my hand on her head while she kept repeating, "The name of

the Lord is a strong tower; I will run to it and be safe."
I grieved until I was sick. I wanted a miracle and not
the trial. I beat down heaven's door until Aaron died
at age four and a half.

Aaron could never see, hear, or respond to
anything except pain. At times he seemed to be a
bundle of blank agony. Aaron had a bushy head of
uncontrollable hair, and onto that head, his parents
put earphones. Aaron heard music, and Aaron heard
the Bible read through twice. When Aaron died, the
Gift that pressure-tested our faith went to be with
his Creator and his God, where he may have been
all along. I went with Ed, Betsy's husband, to select
a cemetery plot. As we went out the door, Betsy said,
"Find a tree." The Lord gave us the last tree in that
Arizona cemetery.

Aaron's life and death raised questions. My faith
had been challenged. Why didn't God heal the
firstborn of an "upright" man and a praying mother?
Why didn't God protect Aaron's birth? Why does
God heal some people and not others? I was not
angry at God. I just wanted to understand. In seeking
to understand, I realized that somehow I wanted God
to prove Himself or be more predictable. God wanted
me to know that I, a fallen child with a finite mind, will
never comprehend His ways. He wanted me to know
that He understands me and my wobbly faith.

When we ask why or say we don't understand, we are reminded of the Last Supper when Jesus sat before His disciples with the bread and the wine and told them a mystery. He told them to eat the bread and drink the wine because it was His body poured out for them. *He did not tell them to understand* or to make sense of His strange request. He said, "Take and eat." They did not understand. There is much we do not understand. The scriptures say God's thoughts are higher than our thoughts and His ways are past understanding. But God says we can know Him. He longs to know us in a personal way. He invites us to contemplate His mysteries and to experience the power of His resurrection and the full measure of His grace.

Faith is a dynamic process. The endurance and strength that comes from pressure-tested faith does not come overnight. Betsy and Ed were not okay all of a sudden because they were Christians and loved the Lord. They grieved and questioned why and to what purpose this deep and lingering pain had been part of their lives. It was by faith they testified that the Most High God was their God. It was by faith they believed that He would lead them through the wilderness to His place of certain good and He would be a light for them in their "valley of the shadow of death" (Ps 23:4 NASB). In the process, from time to time, God gave

Ed and Betsy small gifts of comfort, a small song of joy.

When Aaron died, Betsy and Ed were in Arkansas visiting me. My sister Shawn called saying she was at Betsy's house because the caregiver had called to tell her Aaron was not doing well. Shawn, a nurse, went to check on Aaron. Then she called Aaron's doctor and Betsy. About ten minutes later, Shawn called again. "Betsy, he's gone." I remember clearly the primordial sounds of parental grief.

We all immediately flew to Phoenix to prepare for a funeral. After the funeral, Betsy and Ed returned to Fort Smith to pick up their van and drive back to Arizona. Along the way, they stopped to eat. Isaac, their two-year-old son, was asleep. Not wanting to wake him, they parked the car in the front of the restaurant bay of windows so they could see him when he awoke. They had just sat down when Isaac popped up and Ed went to get him.

When he got settled in the high chair, he had a strange look on his face and Betsy asked him if he was all right. He said, "I just saw brudder." Obviously, Isaac had a dream. "What was brother doing?" Betsy asked. "He was running and singing and playing," Isaac replied. Isaac's dream was a comfort, a reminder of what is truly real behind the veil. Every once in a while, God draws the curtain and lets us see. He gives us reminders that though we are tethered to this earth there is another realm of reality just as real. Every once in a while, He lifts the veil. He thins the space between heaven and earth. He lets us experience the "thin place." He helps our faith.

Storm Exposed

I

A *bruised reed* He will not break
And a *dimly burning wick* He will not extinguish.
—*Isaiah 42:3 NASB (italics added)*

II

Father,
I feel like a flickering wick in the wind
I am poor in spirit and prone to stray
But You, O Lord, bless the poor in spirit
You say that Goodness and Mercy
Follow Your sheep, even when they wander
And You call them by name, even when they are lost
And they know Your voice, even
When they know nothing else.

Your voice is like a gentle, rolling thunder
It reminds me that my heart is deceitful
And the *heart* is the *heart* of the matter.
Unlock my self-guarded, reed-bent, broken, secret
   places
Dismantle my walls of self-deception
Search the deep resources of my being
Control the center and the corners of my mind
Let Your light shine, shine in a humbled heart.

Shine in this one who is poor in spirit,
Who perseveres under trial and
Whose faith is pressure-tested.
Prevail when my candle is storm-exposed
Raise up the fragile reed
When I bend beneath the gale.
Remind me of what I know:
God will not break a bruised reed
Or extinguish a flickering wick
God will stand between the wick and the wind
And lift up the one who bows beneath the load
God will ignite my flame again
I will shine as a Light in the night
I will shine and bless the poor in spirit.

Thin Places

In the Celtic tradition, a "thin place" is the place where the veil that separates heaven and earth is nearly transparent. It is a place where we experience a deep sense of God's presence in our everyday world. A thin place is where, for a moment, the spiritual world and natural world intersect. There are moments when we do feel the divine breaking through into our world. We feel unified and connected with God. It is not an intellectual knowing, it is felt in the spirit. It can be a sudden momentary awareness or profound unexplainable experience. I would like to share a few "thin place moments" with you and encourage you to have *eyes to see* the gifts of thin places.

The phenomenon of a place where the physical and natural everyday world merges into a thin line is well rooted in biblical history, but it was the Celts who first gave the descriptive phrase "thin place" to it. I first understood the idea of thin places when I heard a minister from Tulsa speak to a group of ear, nose, and throat surgeons in Washington, D.C. His point was that he as a minister and they as physicians were in a unique and privileged position to witness "thin places" because both the physician and the clergy dealt in the realm of life and death. He gave an indelible example of one of his experiences.

He said he had been called to the hospital to pray for a dying woman who was in a deep coma. He went in and although she would not be able to know or respond to his presence, he went over and stood at the foot of her bed and prayed for her aloud. He began, "Our Father, who art in heaven . . ." About midway through the prayer, the woman, without waking up, began to join in with him: "Give us this day our daily bread . . ." She finished the prayer and died shortly thereafter. He knew he stood on the line of a thin place.

Another example was told to my husband and me by his senior partner when his wife died. She was in the hospital and the family had been called in because her death was imminent. As Charles and his two children sat by her side, she left her body in the early morning hours. Sherard, the daughter, said to her brother, "Chuck, did you see it?" He said, "What? I did not see anything." She then asked, "Daddy, didn't you see it?" He said, "No, baby, I didn't see anything." She said, "Just as mother died, I saw a mist rise from mother's body, float to the ceiling, and disappear." Sherard witnessed a thin place.

Thin places come in different ways and some can be subtle. I call them "Garden of Eden moments" because they remind me of the way things must have been in the Garden of Eden when the earth was perfect and at peace. I think we have all experienced them, kind of a time of unified joy. The bounty and beauty of nature can bring such joy: a sunrise or sunset, the coming of spring, or a deep winter snow.

Moments of a unified spirit can also come within relationships. One such Garden of Eden moment came when Paul and I went to Disneyworld with our children and grandchildren. After a long day of activity at the park, we headed back to our hotel room on the bus. Paul was sitting next to me with his arm around the back of the seat touching my shoulder. Across from us were our two sons and their wives, talking quietly and content with each other. Their children were curled up, lying in their laps and cradled in the crook of their arms. For one brief moment, I experienced the way it must have been in the Garden of Eden when peace and joy ruled, when all was perfect and everything was the way it should be.

We all have moments of thin places. They are holy places if we just pay attention and let our spirits see. Elizabeth Barrett Browning said:

Earth's crammed with heaven
And every common bush afire with God;
But only he who sees takes off his shoes.

I believe I had a less than subtle thin place experience when I went back to graduate school. Most days, I drove seventy miles to northwest Arkansas to attend the University of Arkansas in Fayetteville. Early on, almost every day, I would wonder what my brain was thinking when I began this task. My brain was rusty, and besides, I was driving a stretch of mountain road that was known for death-producing accidents. I remember questioning if this had anything to do with God's will for my life. I reasoned that I could be using my time doing something more for Him or more beneficial to others.

Then one day I was coming out of a history class and heading across campus. I was somewhat protected under my umbrella but the rain was coming down in sheets and I was wading through puddles of standing water trying to navigate to my next class. When I was almost there, I saw a young man under a tree, sitting on a bench. His umbrella was propped up beside him, and despite the shelter of the tree, he was getting soaked. His clothes were wet and he sat with his wet head in his hands, sobbing, his shoulders shaking hard.

I slowed down and sloshed across the muddy grass and went over to him. I asked, "Can I help you?" He shook his head no. I thought about just walking away, leaving him to his private moment. But I stood there a second and said, "Can I pray for you?" He nodded yes. I placed my hand on his shoulder and said a very short prayer. He never moved, never looked up. He just said, "Thank you."

I walked off and left the young man on the bench in the pouring rain. When I arrived at my building and headed up the steps, I turned around to look at him once again. He was gone. I did not see him walking away. He was just gone. I turned and walked to my class. But I was mystified. My thoughts were, *Where did he go?* Then I wondered if maybe he was an angel. Then I thought, *Maybe I was his angel?* I did not know. All I knew was that I had experienced a special moment that had a meaning, a thin place.

As I thought about the experience, the Lord began to speak. He reminded me that His work is everywhere, and everywhere we are, in every situation, He has plans for us if we have eyes to see. God reminded me He is not just in some planned "spiritual" activity but He is in the everyday sacred mundane of our appointed days.

It is in the flatlands of our everyday routine that we need to remember our thin places. We need to be aware that God has spoken and still speaks. Remembering is one of our greatest challenges. We forget too easily.

C.S. Lewis addresses this tendency to forget in *The Chronicles of Narnia*. In the book *The Silver Chair*, Aslan, the Christ figure, sends Jill and her friend Eustace on a mission. The last words Aslan speaks to Jill as he sends her on her journey is about remembering the *signs* or spiritual truths and heeding a warning not to forget what she learned on the mountain:

Here on the mountain I have spoken to you clearly. I will not often do so down in Narnia. Here on the mountain, the air is clear and your mind is clear; as you drop down into Narnia, the air will thicken. Take great care that it does not confuse your mind. And the signs which you have learned here will not look as you expect them to look, when you meet them there. That is why it is important to know them by heart and pay no attention to appearances. Remember the signs and believe the signs. Nothing else matters.

—C. S. Lewis
The Chronicles of Narnia: The Silver Chair

We are graced with thin moments from time to time, some profound, some subtle. They sneak up on us. So let us keep our eyes open for the gifts of the thinning of the veil as we walk on the mountains. And then let us remember the truths in the flatlands and in the valleys.

Encounter

Everyday courage has few witnesses.
But yours is no less noble because no drum beats
for you and no crowds shout your name.
—*Robert Louis Stevenson*

I

When rivers of fear
From nowhere appear
Without source or direction,
   Encounter me, Lord, high and lifted up
As the flat feeling of emptiness invades,
Suffocating purpose—defying reason,
   Encounter me, Lord, high and lifted up
When anxieties flurry like flocks of restless birds
Let my fluttering sparrow soul

Find the eagle's steady flight
  High and lifted up.
Let me rise to the dwelling place of praise
Hide me—Cover me—
  Encounter me.
Despair has found a harbor
And I cannot lift its anchor
Or send it out to sea;
But I put my trust in You, Lord, to
  Encounter me high and lifted up.

II
I put my trust in you, Lord;
"For those who wait upon the Lord
Shall be renewed
They will take wings like eagles."
High and lifted up.
—*Isaiah 40:31 NIV*

David described his depression as feeling like a "cast" sheep, a sheep that had rolled over on its back with its feet in the air, losing its center of gravity. The sheep would struggle, struggle to "right" itself. It would flail frantically in fear, trying to flip its feet back onto the ground, trying to get itself once again in balance. But the sheep would have to wait for help, wait for someone to turn him right side up. David said, "O my God, my soul is cast down within me" (Ps 42:6 KJV). David felt like a cast sheep, a helpless, stranded, wool-encumbered sheep trying, with all it had, to join the flock on the hill.

David describes his anguish. In Psalm 31:9–10, he says he cries and sighs all the time. He has run out of strength. Sometimes he describes himself as being in great distress. The Hebrew translation for distress describes the feeling of being "bound, cramped, or pressed hard upon."

Depression has sometimes been described as "the dark night of the soul." Winston Churchill called his depression the "Black Dog." This is the same Churchill who rallied the war effort and said, "Never give in, never give in, never, never, never, never . . ."

The depths of a severe depression remain a mystery although there are various causal explanations such as stress, exhaustion, a sense of guilt, loss of a loved one or loss of a job, or a financial setback. There can also be a chemical imbalance of the brain. When some chemicals are low or the delicate balance of chemicals are not working correctly, medication can be very helpful.

Seeking treatment does not announce that you have a lack of faith but rather it indicates that you have a willingness to take advantage of what God has made available through modern science, just as you would for any other illness.

Severe depression is often beyond description—deep and painful feelings of guilt, alienation, and hopelessness plague the thought process. They are like poison arrows to the spiritual being. When we try to read our Bible or pray, there is a lack of concentration and the message can seem meaningless, the words flat. Deep depression is the embodiment of emotional suffering.

Clinical depression affects over nineteen million adults in the United States. It affects all ages, races, ethnic groups, and religions. Christianity is not an exception. It affects millions of Christians. People who are suffering from depression populate our pews. It is not a sign of weakness and many times we cannot just "will" or pray ourselves out of a depressed state. When we experience depression or know someone who has, we know that sometimes its teeth cannot be removed easily. Professional help is needed. Sometimes a pastor can help. Sometimes we need a counselor or a psychiatrist who is able to diagnosis both medical and mental causes. Getting the right person is important. The best counseling harmonizes with our own values and basic beliefs. Whatever the cause of our depression, there is help and hope. The gray veil will lift.

There is counseling and there is medication; but in times like these, our anchor is in our faith in God, God's Word, and in the Good Shepherd who keeps a watchful eye and rescues His "cast" sheep. Never, never, never give in, never. God is good and God loves us.

III

O my soul, why be so gloomy and discouraged?
Trust in God!
I shall again praise him for his wondrous help;
he will make me smile again,
For he is my God!
—*Psalm 43:5 TLB*

Nunnery Ruins at Iona, Scotland: Dedicated to the Sisters of Mercy

I

In 564, Saint Columba left Ireland and sailed with twelve friends to seek God's favor and guidance. They landed off the coast of Scotland and settled on a wildly pagan island called Iona. Rome had fallen and the night of the barbarians was closing in on the space and order of civilization. The early Church of Rome had lost its spiritual life in the cogs of organization. The time had come for a small fellowship of monks to set up a community of light on the dark island of Iona.

In 1208, the community was expanded as a nunnery was built and an order of Benedictine nuns joined the great endeavor to save and evangelize civilization. Their commitment was to change the world with a spirituality that first changed the heart. Their vision was the redemption of a fallen world.

I visited the island of Iona several years ago and walked among the sacred spaces of the nunnery. I entered through a gate along a half-standing stone wall. Cloistered in silence, the skeleton of the nunnery was all that remained; bones of stones, no fleshed-out history, no markers with particulars; just one stone upon the other mortared together, sturdy and fallen. Still standing were stone doorways, arches, columns, and the front of the church. Some of the walls were jagged nubs coming out of the ground; some were half walls, while some had escaped the ruin of time and stood triumphant against a gray sky.

The stones were black and gray as one would expect. But there were surprises of pale pink granite from time to time. Heavy moss and delicate white flowers lined the ledges and grew out of the ancient rocks. On the ground lay the exposed medieval flooring, the same flat stones that were brushed by a nun's long black habit. As I walked among the place of saints and stones, I could not help but think this was a sacred place, a place where prayer and contemplation permeated the day and night, a place where from time to time heaven and earth met and merged into a thin place.

When I asked the local residents about the nuns who lived there, they said they were not familiar with much information about the nuns or the nunnery. Often time during the Middle Ages, nunneries were comprised of women who became nuns for several different reasons. Some, if not most, felt they were "called" to give their life to the Church and to live in small communities serving God. But there were also women who were displaced because of the death or abandonment of their husband or some family situation. They would come and find protection and purpose in the company of a small group of women.

History records very little about the nunnery at Iona or the nature of these women or even who they were. So, as I walked through the ruins, I wondered about these brave, visionary, pioneer women who stepped forward to venture into the adventure of a little community that changed the world.

The work is still being done by churches and the intimacy and impact of Bible study groups, home fellowships, small communities, and the friendships of commitment that are forged within them. Sometimes we wonder if the Church has lost its impact, its power; but throughout history, communities of believers rise to display Christ's love and His redemptive power. When we witness this, we take heart and know the "Church Triumphant" is continually alive and rising from the ruins.

One such community of the committed is the Benedictine Order of the Sisters of Mercy, whose legacy includes the nuns of Iona.

II

Redeemed and Rising from the Ruins

"Not much known or written about it," the locals say.
I follow a grass-bent path to the north gate, open the
  latch, slip into the only evidence-envelope of Iona's
  thirteenth-century nuns.
A fat gray cat ambles across a moss-laden wall.
A flood of fog begins to pull the sky down
  thinning the horizon.
The slender song of a wren breaks into the front edge
  of my morning and random thoughts arise about
  the women who came to these white linen shores
  and hummed rosaries among these stones.
Mary? Margaret? Elizabeth?
What did you fear?
What irresistible "call" wooed you
To the feet crags of the sea?
Did you flinch when
A Divine tool chiseled the shape of humility and
  resilience?
What habits of the heart did you cover,
What face-offs between flesh and spirit?
Did you feel the stir of a woman's body? longings?
  wandering heart?
Or was your Desire consummated long ago in a
  virgin's womb,

Faithful, enough, more than enough, the Desire of
   your heart?

Did you see God in the winter gale,
Or did the mere whine of wind
Send you inside yourself?
Did you detect "signs" in small happenings
And find worship in the sacred mundane?
Did you see beyond your grass-bent path
  to the front edge of Eden's mourning
      to the Fall and the Great Need
  and then the shining of The Grand Plan:
One stone upon the other, mortared together
Sturdy and fallen
Redeemed and rising from the ruins.

I Went into Your Sanctuary and Thought

There are times when we feel spiritually flat. We want to feel different. We want to feel full of praise. We want to feel joyful but we are spiritually dry like parched, cracked ground. Sometimes we can identify a challenge, a trial, or a burden that is making us feel a certain way. But other times we can't put our finger on the root cause of our discouragement. There are times when we are nagged by "feelings." But be assured that God knows us, and His love for us does not depend on our "spirituality" or our performance. We also should rest in the fact that our feelings are fickle. We all have ups and downs. We are emotional beings. This is part of life. But can we do anything to get out of a funk? Can we dial up different thoughts? Can we change our feelings? Many times, we can.

Not too long ago I came across a verse in 1 Samuel 30. The chapter talked about a time when David was defeated by his enemies, rejected by all those around him and discouraged to the core. In verse 6, it says, "But David strengthened himself in the Lord his God" (NASB). How do we strengthen ourselves in the Lord? I believe we do what a verse in Psalms suggests: "Then one day I went into your sanctuary and meditated" (Ps 73:17 TLB). We strengthen ourselves in the Lord by going into His presence and letting Him guide our thinking. Many of the Psalms tell us that David worshipped and meditated on the scriptures. This was no exception. He received new purpose, vision, and authority. He waited patiently to become king.

When we meditate on the scriptures, God encourages us, imparts life to His Word, and gives us perspective. For example, one time I was thinking on a verse in Matthew 18:21–22 about forgiveness. It was when Peter asked Jesus how many times he should forgive when he is sinned against. Peter thought maybe seven times was being generous. Jesus replied seventy times seven. Forgiving one time is hard enough for us, but seventy times seven? That seems a bit much. But Jesus' point was that we should have a forgiving spirit, a forgiving attitude. We are to forgive in the same measure that Christ forgives us—in full measure. Why? It's God's way. Unforgiveness makes us a slave to another person. Did you ever notice how much emotional energy we expend on those we don't forgive? It's like we give them free rent in our head.

As I mulled the verse over in my mind, it suddenly dawned on me, maybe we are supposed to forgive the same sin seventy times seven. It's not a onetime deal. That makes it even more of a challenge. Forgive over and over and over again? Let go of it? Yes, God is able to deal with another person. I concluded that Jesus was telling us, "Yes, it's hard for you to forgive but I've had mercy on you and forgiven you over and over again and you must do the same. And you will need two things: My grace and your choice." You will be set free, but beyond that, God will give you wisdom on how to best deal with difficult situations or relationships. We can weep but we cannot get bitter.

David strengthened himself in the Lord by meditating on the scriptures. Whether on the fields tending his sheep, or in battle fighting his enemy, or reigning on his throne, David poured out his heart to God in worship, meditation, and prayer. He did this whether he was in danger or whether he was discouraged or joyless. He did it despite his feelings. He made a choice to meditate on God's Word.

Meditation is a vital tool for strengthening our self in the Lord. *When our focus changes, our thoughts follow—and then our feelings.* When we go to the Lord's sanctuary and think, He encourages us and teaches us. He deposits His Word in our heart and our mind. And sometimes, sometimes we have a thin place. God is good and God loves us.

I

Then one day I went into your
sanctuary and meditated.
—*Psalm 73:17 TLB*

II

Lord,
Lead me into Your sanctuary
Where I take courage and my dust-born
thoughts are silenced
Where Your Word centers the
   meditations of my mind
And Your Spirit examines the motivations
Of my most inward part.
Incline my spirit to holiness and
   "heaven's will on earth."

III

Counsel me on my glorious destiny and
Remind me that I do not walk on a slippery path
Or stand on a water-soaked sandy cliff.
I am anchored in the Rock of my Sovereign Lord
In the shelter of a most high mountain
In the sanctuary of unseen evidence
Where thoughts are clarified and courage renewed.

II

NO OTHER STREAM

Pressure-Tested Faith:
A Journey

I

"Are you not thirsty," said the Lion.

"I'm dying of thirst," said Jill.

"Then drink," said the Lion.

"May I—could I—would you mind going away while I do?" said Jill.

The lion answered this only by a look and a very low growl. . . .

"I daren't come and drink," said Jill.

"Then you will die of thirst," said the Lion.

"Oh dear!" said Jill, coming another step nearer. "I suppose I must go and look for another stream then."

"There is no other stream," said the Lion.

—C. S. Lewis
The Chronicles of Narnia: The Silver Chair

II

The storm was over. What seemed like an endless weather delay at Raleigh-Durham Airport was really only three hours. My husband and I were returning from a golf vacation at Pinehurst. We were content to be heading back home, back to the foothills of the Ozark Mountains in Arkansas. My husband, Paul, adjusted his seat, leaned back, and announced that he was "all golfed out." I rolled my eyes and smiled. I knew better. It was for good reason that the doormat outside the back entry to our house reads "A Golfer and a Normal Person Live Here."

The plane bumped through its ascent and smoothed out as it flew above a steel-gray blanket of clouds. As we settled in, I adjusted my postage-stamp pillow and leaned my head against the hard surface of the window. I began to float in and out of a light doze. I was awake enough to feel Paul's hand reach over for mine and hear him say, "I love you, girlfriend."

The tender gesture triggered my thoughts. They began to travel ironically to the turbulent times of our marriage, to the stomach-dropping anxiety of a marriage falling apart and all the possibilities that entailed. As the hard memories roamed around in my head, my thoughts fell to the "Center" that had held me together, the God of my faith. I thought about the faith that learns more about God in the storm than it does in the sun, the faith that is pressure-tested in the time and space of living.

I remember the Saturday afternoon when Paul decided he wanted a divorce. I felt as if the center of my being had been smashed against the wall in one short second. I felt needy and broken, angry and fearful, devoid of the faith that God was in control of my life. I did not know that brokenness was the first step to an enlightened heart. I did not know that forced dependence on God can be a "good thing."

It was cold outside and a pewter-gray sky spit a steady mist. I got into the car and mindlessly drove, ending up on a dead-end road, in front of a sign that read "ARKLA Sand and Gravel." I turned off the motor and stared at the mounds of gravel, sand, and rocks. The gray of the day and the sand and the quarried rocks seemed to smother me. I looked at the freshly crushed mountain of rocks and thought about my marriage. My mind smiled at the irony of me ending up at a rock and gravel pit contemplating a "rocky" marriage, a marriage "on the rocks."

I went home and sat on the couch in our comfortable house, a house perched on the high side of a hill, a house that we were assured when we bought it was safe because the foundation had been sunk into the side of the mountain. I sat there and began to doubt the word of the builder. This house could shift. It could slip down the mountain. It could be pulled right off of its moorings by a tornado.

On that early December day, I sat on the couch and looked at the Christmas tree. I saw our life, our marriage hanging on the tree. There were the plain gold and green balls we bought the first year we were married. There were the brightly colored yarn-woven ornaments we picked up in Mexico one year. There were snowmen and gingerbread men I had made out of felt when I experienced a craft-crazed year. Then, of course, there were the children's ornaments: trees, angels, and candy canes cut out of construction paper and Elmer-glued with red, green, and gold glitter.

I don't know how long I looked at the tree before my blank stare shifted to the presents perfectly wrapped and strategically placed under the tree. I remember thinking that the boxes held nothing of value—no "thing" of value. A box cannot hold anything of real value. I had spent so much time wrapping so many boxes of nothing. I wanted to take all of those stupid boxes, walk out on the deck, and toss them as far as I could down the hill.

In the early dark of the winter nights, I drove by fully lighted houses, alive with activity, smoke curling from the fireplace. I'd imagine that all was well in those lighted houses. But where I lived, despair and loneliness grabbed me by the neck, in the dark. I felt depressed to the bone; alone, it seemed, to my very center.

But I was not alone. I had several friends who ministered to me with their prayers and their presence. This was God's provision. There is a scripture that says every good and perfect gift comes down from the Father above. Friends that you can count on in times of need are one of God's "perfect gifts." In fact, one winter night, three friends came over to spend the night with me. We prayed, we ate, and we found time to laugh. I was "lightened" by their presence.

One clear winter night, I lay in bed looking out the sliding glass doors of my room. For the longest time, I looked down at the lights of the city. I thought, *God, how do You keep track of everyone?* I went to sleep looking up at the stars and thinking there was so many stars and so far away. Sometime in the middle of the night, I sat straight up in bed. I had awoken myself up singing "Amazing Grace, how sweet the sound." God had given me a thin place. I felt close to God. I thought, *I don't know how, but He does keep track*. I was not alone.

Somewhere inside of me, there was a spot, a space, indefinable, undefeatable, and unexplainable, a spirit space that could not be quenched by time or circumstance. In all of us is a space not of our own making, but God-placed. It is a place that God wants to enliven with Truth and Faith—truth about ourselves and truth about Him. It is a space that He wants to enlarge with a faith that goes beyond mere learned words, to a relationship. It is a space that God wants stripped of insecure pretentions and man-devised God-assumptions. It is a thirsty place. He wants us to fill it with the Spiritual Truth that God is good and God loves us. Sometimes the space is as small as a grain of mustard seed. But that is large enough for all the light we need for one step, for one day at a time.

There is a tendency for most of us to want God to be a "quick fix." He chooses to be a "slow cure." For example, for the first several months, my claim on God's sovereignty was that He would change my circumstances. I began by wanting what I wanted. I wanted this "thing" to go away. I wanted the broken pieces of my marriage to be glued back together again. I did not want the pain or the reality of the situation.

He did not answer my "do it now" prayer. Instead, He began to enlarge my faith; not that I would get what I wanted but that no matter what happened, no matter what, He would be with me. He would supply my needs; give me good gifts, treasures hidden in darkness.

He began to show me, slowly and sweetly, my shortcomings, my sins, my log in my own eye. Sometimes it was painful but never without consolation. I had to believe I could only work on myself and not anyone else and God was doing a work.

A couple of years ago, our house got a water leak. The hardwood floors on the entire downstairs level were water damaged. The finish was ruined and the wood was buckled. I dreaded what I knew needed to be done. It would be a messy, necessary process. The floors had to be sanded down to the bare wood, the bumps ground down until they were smooth. Then a new finish had to be applied to protect the floor. The process disrupted our lives but there were no shortcuts, no other way to fix it. Sometimes our lives are disrupted while God works on the floors of our heart, removing and replacing boards, grinding and refinishing.

David, his heart ground to dust, said, "A broken and a contrite heart, O Lord, you will not despise" (Ps 51:17 NASB). The classical term for the word "broken" is "contrition." It is taken from the Latin word meaning, "to wear down or grind to pieces." In the messy grinding process, we only see the mess; God sees the finished product. I thought I would die but I didn't. I got my spiritual floors refinished.

A faith journey is not a smooth, linear path. There are times we get weary and worn down. There are times we search for God and wonder if He has hidden behind a tree or crawled under a rock or wandered into a far-off cave. On occasion, we call to God and it seems as if He has lost His voice or refuses to respond. Our cries echo in our ears. It seems that our prayers hit the ceiling and fall back on our head. These times are okay. These are the times we live totally by faith. And if we, like Robert Browning, "stoop into the dark, it is but for a time." My mother used to always say, "Margaret, you will be all right, and, honey, this too shall pass." When our faith seems thin and threadbare, we keep holding onto the sturdy cord of God's faithfulness and claim God's goodness within the mystery of His sovereignty.

We can also take comfort from friends and fellow pilgrims, pilgrims who have gone before us whose eyes could not see and whose feet got weary. We stand in the valley with the prophet Ezekiel among the scattered bones, the dry, disconnected bones. When asked if the bones would ever live again, Ezekiel responded to God's mystery with, "Lord, you alone know the answer to that" (Ez 37:3b TLB).

The answer for Paul and me was that God turned our hearts back toward each other. We turned our will toward commitment. Our coming back together was not easy. We were broken. Our marriage had a fissure in it, like a giant fault line. We needed help. We went to counseling. We both tried hard. It was work and there was work to be done. We had our faith in God's everlasting love.

I do not know why some marriages make it and others do not. I suspect it has to do with our choices. Sometimes we are moved along by our own will and sometimes by the will of someone else. What I know is that God loves us and God is good. I know that God is faithful and our times are in His hands. Over the years, I have learned that God's heart leans earthward toward His beloved. He seeks to reconcile our relationships to one another and to Himself through His Son, Jesus Christ. The work of reconciliation and restoration is the crux of the Gospel message. God longs for us to seek Him and develop a personal relationship with Him. In this personal relationship, God speaks to us through His Spirit and His Word.

Our future is one of hope and infinite possibilities. A couple of years ago, my husband gave me a card. On the front it said, "A Love Story." When I opened it, it read, "Together, Forever. The End." In a way, that card sums up our relationship with God. Life is short. Written between the lines there is joy, sorrow, and a lot we don't understand. But life is a love story between us and God, together forever with no end.

III

TEARING OFF THE MASK

Adversity and the
Character of Faith

Look to a man in the midst of doubt and
danger and you will learn in his hour of adversity
what he really is . . . *the mask is torn off
and reality remains.*
—*Lucretius, Roman philosopher (italics added)*

My mother sat in her peach recliner. She was
working on a crossword puzzle and dressed
in an old pink and yellow, nylon, "over the head"
dress. I sat on the orange, flowered couch that she
had reupholstered a million years ago. I put my
book down, paused a minute, and said, "Mother, if
you could tell me anything that you knew for sure,
what would you tell me?" She looked up and within
a couple of seconds said, "Margaret, if you lose your

faith, you lose everything." I did not say anything. We each went back to our book and crossword puzzle. But I never forgot what my mother said she knew for sure.

Not too long after that, I was reading a story in *Investor's Business Daily*. It featured a man called Everett Alvarez, Jr. He was the first American pilot shot down over North Vietnam and was the longest held prisoner of war during the Vietnam conflict. He spent eight and a half grueling years as a POW. He came to the same conclusion that my mother did: faith is a sustaining power. It has been said that a man without faith needs something to sustain him. Alvarez also concluded that we learn in the hour of adversity. We learn it can tear our mask away and reveal our character and the character of our beliefs.

Alvarez spent the first year and a half in solitary confinement. The enemy wanted to control his mind and break his will. He was caged in a room where rats roamed the floor and crawled into the bed. He was fed dead birds, soup made out of sewer-water, and rice laced with roaches.

He rarely received mail. He did, however, get the letter from his mother telling him that his wife had divorced him. He was subjected to hours of boredom interrupted by periods of sheer terror. But he said the hardest part was being alone and experiencing the pervading sense of loneliness. He said he did a lot of talking to God. He realized he was not alone. The character of faith emerged as the mask was torn off.

He did things like paint the outline of a cross on a stucco wall. He added the words, "Lord, I am not worthy, but only say the word and I will be healed." This was not a cry for some grand deliverance. It was a humble submission and reliance on God's power and sovereignty. He combed his memory for the Catholic Mass, from his days as an altar boy. He searched his mind for childhood memories and pieces of prayers and hymns.

When he was put with other POWs, they all organized themselves and set standards for behavior. They depended solely on each other in terms of values and beliefs. Those who were self-centered were the ones who ended up collaborating with the enemy or not surviving. They learned that the crucible of adversity tested, formed, and revealed their character. It tore off the mask.

After eight and a half years, Alvarez was released from captivity. He went to night school, earned a law degree, served two senior posts in the Reagan administration, wrote two books, and became a successful businessman. How did he survive? He said he credits his survival and his success to God's purpose and his faith.

Everett Alvarez is an example of the power of character, determination, and faith. I have learned that adversity is often a path to truth. It removes the material props and spiritual pretentions that we hide behind. It mutes our "God-talk." It leaves us clothed only in the reality of our core beliefs, whatever they may be. Adversity, if we let it, has a work to do. Quite often, it prepares us for a future task.

Adversity, when we are swimming in the middle of it, challenges the consistency of our behavior. It examines us. It tests us to see if what we believe to be true will stand in the storm. It also tests whether we will stand in the storm for what we say we believe to be true. It tears off the mask to see what is underneath. The book of James speaks to the transformational value of walking the difficult path of adversity and the value of faith:

Consider it a sheer gift, friends,
when tests and challenges come at you from all sides. You know that under pressure, your faith-life is forced into the open and shows your true colors.
So don't try to get out of anything prematurely.
Let it do its work so you will become mature and well-developed, not deficient in any way.
—James 1:2–4 The Message™

Commander of the Heavenly Armies

I

Lord,
Let me rise above the battle
You are my Rock and my Defender.
In You I trust. You are my Fortress
And ready help in time of need.
Lift my spirit above the cadence of marching drums.
Place it in the balm of Your presence where
I rest and You carry my burden.
Lift my spirit high and gently, Lord.
Let me abide in Your strong love and gentle care.
Bathe me in Your presence
And pour over me new strength.
Lift my spirit above the circumstance
You are Lord of Hosts, Commander of the Heavenly
  Armies

You are my hope and my deliverer.
In You I trust.

II

Blessed are those whose help is the God of Jacob
whose hope is the Lord his God. . . .
He upholds the cause of the oppressed
and gives food to the hungry.
The Lord sets prisoners free,
the Lord gives sight to the blind,
The Lord lifts up those who are bowed down,
the Lord loves the righteous.
The Lord watches over the foreigner
and sustains the fatherless and the widow.
—Psalm 146:5, 7–9 NIV (italics added)

In Good Hands

My friend Suzie once told me to go home and bake some chocolate chip cookies. It was an out-of-place suggestion. It took a moment for me to understand that she *really* meant it. Had she heard me? I had been talking about being overwhelmed with doubt, fear, and uncertainty. I had been talking about a "hopeless" situation. My husband and I were separated, and I was thrown into a space that was fearful and unfamiliar. I had been talking about God and wondering if He knew what was going on in my life. And if He *knew*, did He *care*?

All of us have doubts that peek around the corners of our mind, doubts that begin to question God's individual care and love, doubts that even question God's existence, doubts as to whether God can really see what is going on in our life and doubts that mock our faith and tell us it's no use to even try.

These doubt-thoughts are unwelcome visitors. They come just when we need God the most or when we need our faith to be the strongest. We often quickly dismiss such thoughts with feelings of guilt and as a lack of faith. Other times, we allow our doubts to grow into skepticism. Despair, unbelief, a sense of futility, and meaninglessness soon follow.

We find ourselves either ignoring our doubts or dwelling on them. Neither approach is particularly courageous. Neither approach rewards us with spiritual growth or the relief of a willing "bended knee" at God's ways or life's mysteries.

So where do we begin to deal with doubts that lurk in the darkness? How do we keep from giving in or giving up?

A couple of years ago, after I had prayed a million words inside out and upside down, it dawned on me: the paradox of surrendering with courage, of simply saying, "Help me, here I am, Lord; help me understand that my times are in Your hands." I later realized that this prayer was the center of my need, the starting place of my peace. Help me understand that my times are in Your hands.

My friend knew that I should not feel guilty for my doubts, nor should I give way to dark thoughts. She knew I needed to face hard questions, look for answers, and be willing to bow before mysteries. She knew I needed to get up, go home, and get on with it. "Go home and bake cookies."

I went home, got out the flour, shortening, sugar, and chocolate chips. I baked some big, fat chocolate chip cookies, put on a smile, poured some milk, and called my boys into the kitchen to a home-baked treat.

I stopped asking for what I did not need at the time—answers of the why, the how, and the what for. I needed but one thing, one prayer; I poured out my heart with my feelings and fears and asked God, *Help me understand that my times are in Your hands.* As David often does in the Psalms, I started out with my deep fears and anxious thoughts, with the uncertainties of the unknown and my despair of the known. I started out lamenting. But as often happened with David, the Holy Spirit came within my prayer and reminded me that He was good and faithful and His promises were bedrock sure.

My Times Are in Your Hands

I

Help me understand . . .
My times are in Your hands
From the beginning to the end
My times are in Your hands.

I am often a butterfly—caught—struggling in a net
Or pinned on a board.
   Scattered thoughts press in on me.
Your promise is to see each crisis of my soul
Hear my whispered plea
Help me understand
My times are in Your hands.

Margaret Wills

At times I am the last leaf twirling
In the wind on a winter's tree.
   Loneliness crowds in on me.
Your promise is
That You are my friend
Hear my whispered plea
Help me understand
My times are in Your hands.

Your goodness is bedrock sure
Your Word is true, regardless of what I feel.
Your promises are Light and Life Giving
   From the beginning to the end,
My times are in Your hands.

II

But I trust in you, O Lord;
I say, "You are my God."
My times are in your hands.
—*Psalm 31:14–15 NIV (italics added)*

Whether or Not

How many times has God heard, "Lord, I can't stand this anymore" or "God, help me get out of this" or "Please, Lord, make this go away"? I have prayed these prayers and interesting variations of them on many occasions. I call them "deliver me" prayers.

I usually pray these prayers in times of adversity or personal crisis. I don't want to face the fire, refiner's or otherwise. I don't want my faith tested. I just want things to be "normal." I ask God to change my situation. "Deliver me."

Sometimes the prayer is on behalf of someone I love. I remember the night our youngest son, Shawn, called to tell us that Amy, his wife, who was pregnant with their first child, had been taken to the hospital ill. She was checked in, and shortly after getting into her room, the baby's heart rate cratered off the monitor.

When we got the call, I could clearly see my physician husband, Paul, sitting down, putting his elbows on his knees, and cupping his hands over his face. He sat there like a statue, knowing what the consequences could very likely be: Either a dead or a brain-damaged baby. How well we knew. Finally, he stood up and said, "Let's go." We flew to Houston. Before we left, we called everyone to pray. I prayed, "Please make this go away."

Upon arriving in Houston, we heard the story: our lifeless baby granddaughter had been born. It was described that she had been born "without life." Her first two Apgar scores (tests for quality of life) were zero. They did every life-saving measure possible. She slowly began to show minimal signs of life. It took ten minutes before the doctors were able to stabilize her. She was put on a respirator. She was alive. We had a miracle. We had a "deliver me" prayer answered. How is Abby now? Abby is now a bright, active, full-of-life ten-year-old. She warms our heart and lights our life. We often look at her and marvel.

The older I get, the less I pretend to know about the workings of God. But I also become more and more sure of two things: God loves me, and God cares more about my faith, my spiritual maturity, and my intimacy with Him than He cares about my comfort.

This I know. One time I was praying one of those "inside-out, upside-down" prayers when suddenly I realized what I really wanted was a guarantee of the future—the future, the way I envisioned it. There is no guarantee. There is just Faith and Grace.

Sometimes, I still pray "deliver me" prayers. But my prayers have expanded to "whether or not" prayers. Whether He changes my circumstance or whether He doesn't, my faith is in Him and not just His deliverance from a specific situation. The object of our faith is always God. The fact of our faith is that God can change anything. God can give Grace for anything. This brings tremendous freedom.

The "Whether or Not Prayer" is the very center of the Bible's account of three Jewish young men, Shadrach, Meshach, and Abednego. The biblical story found in Daniel, tells how King Nebuchadnezzar erected a ninety-foot-tall, gold image of himself and ordered all of his subjects to bow down and worship it.

All three of the young men refused. As a result of their defiance, they were threatened to be burned alive, thrown into a furnace heated up seven times hotter than normal. They stood their ground and were led into the hot blast of the furnace. The story tells of a great miracle. Only their bindings burned, otherwise not a hair on their head was singed. God had protected them and delivered them from the fire.

This is an example of God's deliverance from a circumstance. But I believe the greater story, the greater miracle, is Shadrach, Meshach, and Abednego's faith in God and their response to the king's last offer of an opportunity to obey his command: bow or burn. God's young servants told Nebuchadnezzar that their God was able to deliver them but whether He did or not, they would not worship the golden image which the king had set up. They knew that God alone was the object of their allegiance and faith. They knew His grace was sufficient in the time of fear and fire.

Faith in the Fire

I

Blessed be the God of Shadrach, Meshach,
   and Abednego—
We all know that God *has not* promised
To spare us *from* the furnace.
Our fiery furnace will come;
Our God is able to deliver. But if not, let it be known:
He is in the fire, He is on the throne
He is in the fire and we will not be burned.
Do not bow to circumstance. Do not turn around.
Only that which binds us will burn.

II

Blessed be the God of Shadrach, Meshach,
    and Abednego—
For we all know: God *has* promised to
    stand with us *in* the furnace
Our fiery furnace will come,
But our God is able to deliver those
    who trust him in their trial
For faith in the fire will serve to confirm
He is able to deliver. He is still on the throne.
How mighty are his wonders. How great is His name.
In the hottest fire, He is in the midst of the flame.
Let it be known:
Blessed be the God of Shadrach, Meshach,
    and Abednego.

III

And without faith it is impossible to please God,
because anyone who comes to him
must believe that he exists and that he rewards
those who earnestly seek him.
—Hebrews 11:6 NIV

IV

THE FALL

The Promise

I

It refuses to leave unseen,
   to let go in some *humble* way. Instead,
It upstages, steals the show—
This season: these leaves
   of glorified red and purified gold.
Each holds tenaciously to the tree,
To a moment, until a winter chill
Or last stiff wind shakes its space and
Turns emboldened blaze to mottled brown

It is the fall that knits the soul to season
And shows the slant of shortened shadows in the sun
   of folded winds on western mountain.

Margaret Wills

In the fall we feel our living,
See the cadence of the years and
The letting go of branches and barren sphere,
In the fall we see by Faith the Promise of the Season:
Grafted Branches, Eternal Leaves
Glorified Red and Purified Gold.

V

SPEAKING IN THE WAVES

Blessed Are Those Who Have Not Seen Yet Believe—Part I

Jesus stood on the up-slope of the mountain and delivered the Sermon on the Mount. He addressed the soul-hungry crowd. He taught about the people who were *really* blessed—not the ones with long robes or long answers or lots of money. No, He blessed the followers who were searching, the ones who were broken-hearted, discouraged, and troubled. They were His students, spread like an apron on the hillside. He was their Teacher. He fed them and bestowed on them blessings.

But there was another time when Jesus pronounced a special blessing on a group of people, people who He saw in the future. I love this blessing because He reached out to you and me and to all those who the Father gave him. He saw us and said, "Blessed are those who have not seen, yet believe" (Jn 20:29 NIV). Yes, He blessed us.

Jesus knew there would be a "faith hurdle" because we could not physically see Him. So, after His resurrection, when His disciple Thomas said he would not believe unless he saw for himself, Jesus accommodated him. He offered him His nail-scarred hands, His feet, and His pierced side. Then Jesus told Thomas not to doubt but to believe. Thomas went from doubt to belief and cried out, "My Lord and my God." At that moment, Jesus saw us. He looked forward into the faith and the doubt of future believers and blessed those who have not seen. He tells us, like He told Thomas, not to doubt but to believe.

To me, it is encouraging that Jesus met *honest* Thomas where his head and his faith were. That is, at his point of questioning and doubt, at his point of need, at his point of naked honesty. Thomas was an eyewitness to the miracle, but Jesus lived the lead role in the Father's plan. We must go to Jesus with our doubts. He is our confirming source.

This story was recorded only in the book of John. It was written at a time when there were few—if any—other, living witnesses. I imagine God wanted us to know that we do not have to be eyewitnesses to believe. We are blessed because we believe without having seen the event in time and space. We are blessed because we have the witness of the Holy Spirit who draws us to Jesus. In *The Silver Chair* by C.S.

Lewis, Aslan says, "You would not have called to me unless I had been calling to you."

We all have moments of doubt. But Jesus meets us at our place of puny faith and carries us to the safe place of belief and sometimes to the sacred place of "My Lord and my God" faith. Blessed are those who believe, yet do not see. God is good and God loves us.

Sheltered Light

I

Your light
Was all I could see
In the night when I searched for hope
And wondered if someone cared enough
To shield a flickering wick
From the wind
My friend.

II

One time, during a "faith crisis," I was ashamed when I confessed the truth to my friend Suzie: I told her that my faith was tired and weak. I lacked enough faith to just . . . *believe*. She looked at me, smiled, and said, "That's all right, Margaret; I'll have faith for you." Samuel Coleridge said that friendship is like a sheltering tree. I needed a shelter. I needed faith. I needed a friend.

Suzie reminded me of the availability of grace and how one time a Roman captain asked Jesus if He would heal one of his prized servants who was on his deathbed. The captain, being a man who understood authority, sent word that Jesus didn't need to come all the way to his house, He just needed to say the word and his servant would be healed. Jesus applauded the centurion's simple faith and healed the servant. (Story found in Luke 7:1–10.)

She also mentioned the faith of the four men who carried their crippled friend to the house where Jesus was healing and teaching. The four friends couldn't get in the front door because of the crowds. So they hoisted their friend up to the top roof and eased him down through a tile opening on the rooftop. Jesus admired the faith of the four men. He told the paralytic his sins were forgiven and to pick his bed and walk. (Story found in Mark 2:1–5.)

Suzie continued, "And then, of course, what about the man who couldn't quite believe that the Lord could deliver his son from an unclean spirit?" The man had gone to Jesus' disciples and they could not help. He then went to Jesus and said, "If you can do anything, take pity on us and help us." Jesus said, "'If you can'? All things are possible to him who believes." Jesus stressed the importance of faith. The man said, "I do believe. Help my unbelief." Jesus healed his son. (Story found in Mark 9:21–24 NASB.)

Yes, that was where I was. I couldn't quite believe *enough*. I needed grace. I needed the faith of a friend who would help me remember the faithfulness of the Lord. Suzie's faith and friendship carried me. My faith was nurtured and encouraged. Henri Nouwen observed:

> In times of doubt or unbelief the
> community can "carry you along," so to speak;
> it can even offer on your behalf what you
> yourself overlook, and it can be the context in
> which you recognize the Lord again.

Visitation

I

There are times when our prayers are simple, not sophisticated; raw, not refined. If we can pray at all, our prayers come from somewhere deep, some primordial groaning. We can hardly catch our breath. They are needy and childlike. If we can mouth anything, it is simply "God" or "help me" or "have mercy." In times like these, we pour out the center of our being, like a river without boundaries. When our heart is broken, God's ears are open. Don't let go of these prayers. Don't let go of God's Word. Don't let go of your faith. Stay with the psalmist who constantly declares the hope and help of the Lord.

II

O Spirit of God
Walk by my side
Abide with me inside
I walk down a strange road
With a heavy load
Down a strange and scary road

All safety is gone
Everything seems wrong
I don't seem to belong
Give heed to lonely cries
Lift my unseeing eyes
Comfort uncontrollable sighs.

III

For I cried to him, and he answered me!
He freed me from all my fears
—Psalm 34:4 TLB

IV

O Spirit of the Living God,
You hear.
You are near.
I raise my hands to You
And give You praise
And give You praise.
I raise my hands to You
And give You praise.

V

I will praise the Lord no matter what happens.
I will constantly speak
of his glories and his grace.
I will boast of all his kindness to me.
Let all who are discouraged take heart.
Let us praise the Lord together, and exalt his name.
—Psalm 34:1–3 TLB

Proofs and Signs

When I was a little girl, before the grown-up year of thirteen, I would ask God to show up so I could see him. I wanted proof. Usually, I would ask for this visitation at night after I had gone to bed. I would lie still and watch the cooler blow gentle waves on my white lace curtains. I would pull the sheets up to the curl of my neck, listen to the silence, and say my prayers. I would ask God to appear (an angel would be fine) at the end of my bed. I would scrunch my eyes closed really tight and start counting; one one-thousand, two one-thousand, three one-thousand, all the way up to fifteen. Then I would open my eyes to the darkness. There would be nothing—zip, nada, nothing at all. No light, no angel, no God. It was still dark. I was still alone. I never told anyone I did this. I knew it was, you know, kind of stupid—asking God to materialize.

Today, I smile about my request for a visual sighting. But I smile also in thinking how God really did show up. I just did not see Him in the way I asked. I now understand that my asking to see Him was the stirring of a real God-placed spiritual need. I was responding, not initiating. God came, not at the end of the bed, but inside of me in the form of a need, a spiritual need and hunger that only He could satisfy. One time God did, in a sense, "stand at the end of the bed." He appeared in human history in the form of a man over two thousand years ago. His name was Jesus. He came that we might know our God.

The wise King Solomon wrote that God has placed eternity in the heart of man. We yearn for spiritual meaning. We just sense there is something more, something apart, something "other" than the material world. It is a God-placed yearning.

So when you ask for a sign or proof or a visitation in the darkness of the night, or in your "dark night of the soul," don't think it's silly. Don't be afraid to ask. Just be willing for Him to come any way He chooses. Just keep your eyes and ears open.

Look at me. I stand at the door. I knock. If you hear me call and open the door, I'll come right in and sit down to supper with you. . . . Are your ears awake?
—*Revelation 3: 20–22 The Message*

This Is the Day for
Walking on the Water

I

This is the day for walking on the water.
Listen to the Lord speaking in the waves,
"It is I. Come, come, walk on the water."
What could be safer than walking on the water?

In the fearful darkness of the night,
In the middle of the storm,
When the sea would be your master
Listen to the voice that says, "Come."
This is the day for walking on the water.

Don't look up at the crashing waves.
Don't look down at your sinking feet.
Keep your eyes stayed on Jesus,
Listen to The Master of the Seas.
This is the day for walking on the water.

Listen to the Lord in troubled waters.
He's speaking in the waves:
"Don't let your heart be troubled,
Neither let it be afraid."
This is the day for walking on the water.

II

But Jesus immediately said to them:
"Take courage! It is I. Don't be afraid."
"Lord, if it is you," Peter replied,
"tell me to come to you on the water."
"Come," he said.
Then Peter got down out of the boat,
walked on the water and came to Jesus.
—*Matthew 14: 27-29 NIV*

VI

A LISTENING HEART

A Listening Heart

What does it mean to have a listening heart? It means to listen to the place within ourselves that is more profound than just an information center. It is the place that is deeper than the mind. It is the place where the ears of the spirit and the will exist. It is the place where we affirm or deny the speaking of God's spirit. It is the place we listen to when we pray for wisdom.

It was the beginning of my last semester of graduate school. I only had to complete the semester and write my dissertation and then I would have my doctoral degree. There was only one major obstacle in my mind and that was the statistics class that I had put off on purpose until the very end. Since math was always my "short suit" (really my short, short suit), I had waited until the last possible moment to subject myself to intellectual humility.

I was apprehensive, but I reminded myself I had taken math classes before and survived. I could manage the challenge. That was until the first day I walked into the long-dreaded statistics class. I was a bit late, and I slithered into the last seat on the third row. While I adjusted myself at my desk, I heard the professor talking and asking questions. I also heard students answering questions and sounding smart as if they knew what they were talking about. I saw the professor writing formulas all the way to the bottom of the blackboard. This went on for about twenty minutes until I began to get that sinking feeling in the pit of my stomach. I was clueless as to the questions and the answers. I scanned the room to see if anyone appeared as lost as I was. Nope. There was no one who looked like they were about to hyperventilate.

My fear started to grow like those multi-colored crystal rocks that expand when you put them into water. I began to think that I was the only one that was going to fail this class. I was in trouble. I was in over my head. I thought I was dead meat in the streets of statistics land. I left class and headed to my car to drive the seventy miles home. I opened the door and let anxiety sit in the passenger seat.

On the way home, I conjured up images of failure. I feared failure and was beginning to feel desperate. I began to pray. I prayed for wisdom. I prayed the "inside-out, upside-down, every which way" prayer. You know the one, the prayer that prays in all different kinds of ways just to be sure to touch all the bases. I remember my most piercing feeling was one of inadequacy. It's a terrible thing to feel inadequate. Most of the time, it's a feeling that has nothing to do with reality. As my sister Shawn says, "You just have a party in your own head."

After a while, I settled down to the quiet of the car. And then a not-too-original thought occurred: *I need a statistics tutor.* Then I thought, *Go by Southside High School and see if a local math teacher will help me.* Was this God talking? I didn't know but I drove the rest of the mountain winding way home and immediately stopped at the local high school. It was late afternoon and most of the teachers were gone. So I wasn't too hopeful when I stopped by the office. But the woman behind the counter directed me to the room of a math teacher.

I walked in and there stood the "sweet angel lady" who would be my salvation—the math teacher. I laid out my pitiful plight. She listened attentively and then spoke to my fear. She said, "I'm sorry. I just don't have the time."

I refused to be denied so I lingered for a while, talking, asking her several more times I thought she might change her mind. After all, I was pretty close to begging. She was sympathetic but she held her ground. Finally, I thanked her and started to walk out. Just then a young woman walked through the door. The math teacher introduced me to Kimberly, her student teacher from the University of Arkansas. She was, of all things, a statistics major. I quickly cut to the chase and asked her the question: "Would you tutor me in statistics?" Was it an accident that she said she would help me? I don't think so. It was God's provision to a desperate prayer from a fearful child who felt anxious and inadequate.

Several years later as I thought about the incident and the answered prayer, I began to think of the value of having a "listening heart." I had been directed to Southside High School where I met someone who would help me.

Oddly enough, I began to think about Solomon when he became king. He was still in his late teens. He got the sinking feeling that he was inadequate. I imagine that he was overwhelmed. In I Kings 3, God appeared to Solomon in a dream and asked him what he wanted. Fearful, Solomon acknowledged that he did not have the talent or the skill to govern a nation. He wisely asked that God grant him an "understanding mind." In Hebrew, the words mean a "listening heart."

I believe inherent in the wisdom that God promises is our acknowledgment that we are dependent upon

Him. I also believe that when we pray for wisdom, we should also be mindful of a "listening heart." Perhaps our thoughts are God leading us, God's way of giving us an opportunity to see Him work. A listening heart is always prompted to obey. This is where wisdom comes in.

How did I do in the statistics class? Kimberly did a great job. We met many times during the semester, during which Kimberly displayed a great deal of patience. I missed an A by two points.

James 1:5 says that if we need wisdom we just have to ask God and He will give it to us without holding back and without criticizing us for asking for it. We all have "wisdom deficiency." There are times when we are acutely aware of this. But God promises to provide wisdom for us. God is good and God loves us. And God loves a "listening heart."

Presumption

I

Lord,
Don't let me put You into a box
Lest You stay there and I get lost
Lest I confine You in my mind
By perfect doctrines of every kind
With "ages" and "stages"
And "pre" and "post" cages
Don't let my "concept" of You
Limit my knowing You
Father, fill me up or empty me
Just be free to work in me.
And like Job, let me see . . .

II

Then Job replied to the Lord;
"I know that you can do all things;
no purpose of yours can be thwarted.
You asked, 'Who is this that obscures
my plans without knowledge?'
Surely I spoke of things I did not understand. . . .
My ears had heard of you but now my
eyes have seen you."
—*Job 42:1–3, 5 NIV*

VII

OUR STARTING PLACE

Faithfulness Is Your
Very Character

I

I look around and there is change:
The movement of seasons, the rise and fall of the tide,
The subtle and sure shift of the ocean's shore,
The blowing of the wind.

Many times, like children, we draw simple,
　　straight lines;
"Change lines." Our "before and after" lines:
Before the diagnosis, before the divorce,
Before the economic earthquake,
Before the death of a loved one.

II

I look around and there is change
I cannot rest in today's safety
For tomorrow . . .
It will slip through my hand
    as sand.
But You, O God, remain the same.
Your promises are sure
Time does not add
    or subtract Your character.
You are patient and merciful
You are forgiving and just.
You are what You always have been
    and You will not change.
I rest mightily in Your faithfulness.

III

O Jehovah,
Commander of the heavenly armies,
where is there any other
Mighty One like you?
Faithfulness is your very character.
—*Psalm 89:8 TLB*

The Teacher

Take my yoke upon you.
Let me teach you, because I am humble and gentle
at heart and you will find rest for your souls.
—Matthew 11:29 NLT

When Jesus spoke, everyone listened. People ran to get their neighbors and friends. Jesus taught in the market place among the shoppers; He stood in boats and taught. He gathered the people on the hillside, delivered sermons, and told stories. He taught how to live the good life and how to be good.

He told those who chose to follow Him to listen to what He said and to learn from Him. He said to the wanderers, "I am the Way." To the seekers, He said, "I am the Truth." To the weary, He promised to carry their burden. He made great claims about Himself:

He said He was the Son of God. He said He could take away their sins. He said He had a Kingdom. He said wise men paid attention to Him, and built their life on His teachings. He said foolish men ignored the truth of what He had to say.

Wherever Jesus went, thousands of people followed Him to hear what He had to say. Crowds gathered around Him, like hungry children. There was excitement and expectation in the air. The educated came; the common folks came. The children came to listen to this man from Galilee who asked questions and told stories, this man who healed the sick, bound up the broken hearted, and set the captive free. He was a wise and different teacher. He taught like someone who had great authority and yet He was simple and humble. For over two thousand years, the world has called Him the Great Teacher. After two thousand years, people still come to hear the words of Jesus.

Jesus taught from the context of our normal everyday life. For example, He would see a tree and say, "A tree is known by its fruit." The character of our everyday life counts. It is our heart-behavior of patience, kindness, humility, respectfulness, forgiveness, honesty, and commitment that is the good fruit. The poet Annie Dillard says, "The way we live our days is the way we live our lives." How do we live our days? Do we follow the teacher? Do we want to change? Do we want to be healed of emotional dysfunction? Do we want to go through the process of spiritual transformation?

Process is a time-word and a time-reality. We are asked to return to God some of the precious gift of our time. He will lead us into exactly what that looks like for each of us. But it is sure to involve obeying Him when He says, "Learn of me." It is sure to involve a humble and teachable spirit. To that end, we have the guidance of both the scriptures and the Holy Spirit. The Holy Spirit is our unseen strengthener, comforter, helper, teacher, and truth giver. We are sterile without the Holy Spirit. We lack knowledge without the scriptures. It is within the challenge of each day that we are called to discipleship, called to be students of Jesus. Discipleship involves, listening, choosing, and changing. Jesus is the Master Teacher.

The Teachings of the King

You call me "Teacher" and "Lord,"
and rightly so, for that is what I am.
—*John 13:13 NIV*

A King was born. He taught about His Kingdom.
He called His people friends, not subjects.
He told them to, "Enter In."
Enter the hard way, the narrow way.
Then He said, "I am the Way. Abide in Me."

He taught them that He was their King.

He taught them to lay down their sword when their
heart cried vengeance
When their heart cried not at all, He taught them to
have eyes to see.

He taught them righteousness instead of the ease of
    expediency.
He taught them the power of a gentle spirit
    the secret force of having ears to hear
        the indomitable strength of washing feet.

He taught them that He was their King.
He taught them to use their mind, their time, and
    their talents but
Not to use their friends, not to misuse their
    relationships.
He taught them to confront and He taught them to
    turn away in silence.
He taught them that their word was their contract
    and that their life was their message.
He taught them that faith cannot operate outside of love.

He taught them He was their king.

He taught them to pick up their cross and the cross
    would interfere with their life.
It would do to them what it did to Him—put the flesh
    to death.
He taught them to be stalks of wheat and then
    warned them there would be look-alike weeds.
He taught them to be good soil, plant good seed, be
    salt and light.

He reminded them that His Kingdom was different
than the world's domain.
He reminded them that they were different.

He taught them that He was their King.

When He left, He left the Gift of the King, the Holy
Promise.
He said, "The Kingdom of God is in you."

Cast the First Stone

I

In John 8, the Scribes and the Pharisees came to Jesus bringing a woman they had caught in the act of adultery. They all stood on the sand together: the shamed adulteress, the demanding Scribes and Pharisees, and the sinless Jesus. The Scribes and the Pharisees pointed to her, reminding Jesus that the Law required an adulteress to be stoned. Jesus remained silent and then stooped down and began to draw on the sand. Finally, He told the person without sin to be the first one to start the stoning. Tight-lipped, they turned around and walked away, leaving the woman standing with Jesus. Jesus asked her where her accusers were. She told Him they were gone, she had no accusers. Jesus said, "I don't accuse you either, go and quit sinning."

In a way, Jesus "killed two birds with one stone": the Pharisees with the hypocritical nature and hidden sins and the woman with the shame and the blatant sins. Neither was without sin. Both had their conscience confronted by Jesus; and both had a choice. Jesus did it with silence and a simple reply: let him without sin be the first to begin.

Jesus wants us to get the point about the dangerous aspect of judging. We are all sinners, and we all have a tendency to point out someone else's faults while overlooking our own.

On another occasion, in Matthew 7:1–5, Jesus warns us about the danger of judging. He says we will be judged by the same measure that we judge. Have you ever noticed how we tend to be harder in our reflexive judgment on someone who has a critical and judgmental spirit, than on someone who gives grace and mercy?

Jesus goes on to ask a question about a log and a speck. Why, He asked, do we have a tendency to see the small speck or splinter in another person's eye and ignore the large log or plank in our own eye? None of us are without faults, and we should take care of our own sin before we criticize others. We are to avoid a narrow, negative, critical, and judgmental spirit. Why? Because it pushes us away from other people, it comes back to us in the same measure we dole it out, and because it keeps us from addressing our own issues and our own sins.

So, like a teacher who wants his students to get the lesson or a parent who wants his child to listen to him, Jesus makes the point in several different ways. He emphasizes that we should not single out other people's sins when we are not perfect and have our own shortcomings to address. I have been guilty more times than I want to admit, and I want to get the point of the stones, the logs, and the specks.

II

They caught her in sin and brought her to him
The Law says, "Stone her," they cried
Jesus stooped down and wrote on the ground
Then he stood and replied,
"If she is alone cast the first stone.
Let him without sin be the first to begin
To cast the first stone."
Silence made a sound as the stones
     dropped to the ground.
With pursed lips, they had nothing more to say
So they turned their backs and marched away.

III

Lord, You taught me to love and forgive
  and to look inside at how I live.
You taught me not to cast stones for only You stand
  alone without sin.
I seek the grace of Your touch as I drop the stones in
  my clutch.
I welcome hands that are free
Without stones.

IV

Let any one of you who is without sin
be the first to throw a stone at her.
—John 8:7 NIV

Blessed Are the Poor in Spirit: The Kingdom of God Is Available

Jesus stood on the mountain, looked out over the patchwork of people, and began to deliver His Sermon of Hope. Like a laser beam, His eyes zeroed in on the slope-shouldered individuals who were "poor in spirit," those who had lost the hope that they would change or that anything about them would ever be any different.

Jesus began to bless them first, as if they had some privileged position, as if their neediness had put them in the front of the line. "Blessed are the poor in spirit, for theirs is the kingdom of heaven," he said (Mt 5:3 NIV). Jesus blessed those who were spiritually bankrupt and spent, out of resources, empty of credentials and religious coins. He blessed those who had reached into their spiritual pockets and found them empty. He blessed those who were turned inside out, upside down in the dark. He blessed those who were desperate, needy, and at the end of their rope. He offered hope. Jesus blessed the poor in spirit and announced the availability of a Kingdom of Hope. Jesus is our starting place.

Starting Place

I

Hemmed in, pinned in, pushed against a wall
No place to go, think I'm going to fall
Pressures from the present, pushes from the past
Can't get it together, don't think I'm going to last.
I can't look inside, don't know myself
What I used to be is high upon a shelf
All is mass confusion, where can I turn
Where are the answers that I feel compelled to learn?

Oh, God, search my spirit and clear my finite mind.
Let me find in You the answers I must find.
Look on me in mercy: I'm pinned against the wall.
Be my starting place as on my knees I fall.

II

"For I know the plans I have for you,"
declares the Lord, "plans to prosper you and not to
harm you, plans to give you hope and a future.
Then you will call on me and come and pray to me,
and I will listen to you. You will seek me and
find me when you seek me with all your heart.
"I will be found by you," declares the Lord,
"and will bring you back from captivity."
—*Jeremiah 29:11–14 NIV*

Get Ready and Wait

I

Get ready to praise the Lord.
His ear has heard my plea
His desire
   was to delight in my request
The answer
   comes on wings of praise.
I wait in quiet trust
   and eagerness
To see the mighty work
He will do on my behalf
For His glory.

II
O God in Zion
we wait before you in silent praise
and thus fulfill our vow.
And because you answer prayer,
all mankind will come to you
with their requests.
—Psalm 65:1-2 TLB

VIII

THE WAY TO YOUR DOOR

The Vine

I

All the trees of the fields are dried up.
Surely people's joy is withered away.
—Joel 1:12 NIV

II

Out of Your Mercy you mend my ways.
Out of Your Love you look upon me.
When I am overwhelmed at my
Wayward heart and feel like
A withered branch
Without spring buds or summer fruit,
I hear Your voice tell me to rest,
Rest
In Your forgiveness.

You guide me
Back
To the cross where I was grafted—
Carefully, lovingly, grafted to the Vine
And introduced to the Vinedresser.

What can I say to a God of Love
Who cleanses my sin and remembers not again?
Confession rights a withered branch
As life flows from the Vine
And confession's tears are the morning dew
On buds that soon will bloom.

III

Though you forget the way to the Temple
There is one who remembers the way to your door.
—*T.S. Eliot*

IX

THE REALITY OF LIVING

Where Else Shall We Go?

Even if awareness of faith has crept in on
silent feet, like the dawn, the daylight reality
of faith requires our full participation.
—*Os Guinness*

There was a time when I yearned to experience the
reality of the Christian faith, not just the words. I
wanted to know God in a more definitive way. I read
books on prayer, faith, and the spiritual disciplines.
All of the books I read had something to say and were
helpful, especially those on the spiritual disciplines.
But what I learned, God taught me, on my own: His
Word generates faith, and God uses our everyday life
as a stage to show up in a very real way.

It is when we choose to depend on Him for the
demands of everyday life that we experience His

faithfulness. It is when we choose to let Him model how we relate to people that He gives grace and love and joy, enough to share. It is when we throw ourselves into His arms in a crisis that we know that He is "better than a light and safer than a known road." Even when God is silent, He is present. God meets us where we live and gives us the best opportunities to experience His reality in faith and answered prayer.

We all want an easy life. We don't want hardship to spoil our days. We don't want to need to trust God. When I am in the foreign land of struggles and troubles, I need the Lord. There is nowhere else to go. I feel like Peter in John 6. When Jesus asked His disciples if they wanted to leave him as so many of His other followers had when the teachings became hard and the road difficult, Peter said, "Lord, to where shall we go? . . . You are the Holy One of God with eternal life." When we are burdened and laden down with troubles, we should turn to the Lord. "The name of the Lord is a strong tower" (Prov 18:10 NASB). We can run to it and be safe. Going through challenging times are difficult. It is not a bed of roses. But God never promised us a rose garden. He promised never to leave us or forsake us.

We must have faith. The Bible says that he who comes to God must believe that He is. I visualize Michelangelo's painting on the Sistine Chapel where there is the picture of man in all his glory and God in all His Glory, both reaching out. Their arms are extended toward each other, their fingers almost, almost, but not quite, touching. To me, the gap represents faith. The bridge between us and God is our faith, faith for our salvation and faith for our daily walk. Our faith in Jesus bridges the gap between us and Him. What challenge are you facing that is an opportunity to experience the reality of God in your life? When you are tired and confused and don't know where to go or what to do, go to Jesus. He will either step into your circumstances or give you grace and peace to walk your appointed path. Jesus came that we might know our God. God is good and God loves us.

A New Song

I

We are all seekers. We seek to know why we are here and the purpose and meaning of our lives. We want to know where we go when we die. We seek to know if there is a God. And if so, what kind of God is He?

Modern culture tells us there are no real answers to these questions. It all just depends on what we think is best for us. It is all relative. We can deceive ourselves if we think there are no absolute answers, but the thought of no answers cannot be lived with; our heart knows better. The quest to answer the questions and the desire for God and for meaning is innate. God placed a space in our heart that only He can fill. It feels like we are hungry and we don't know what we want. We can taste many things like success, wealth, fame, material possessions, or sensual pleasures. But in the end, they all wear thin and wear out. They all come up empty. Jesus said He came to give us eternal life and abundant life. The Bible says that Jesus is the exact image of the invisible God. Jesus came that we might know who God is and what He is like.

II

I often fly to the sun and
  ride the falling stars.
My mind sits on the mountains,
  and the trees
  and the eons of time.

I know
I am a passing part of it all.
I hear soft winds . . . wild winds . . .
  saying
      Life is too close to living.
      Feeling good is too close to hurting.
      Having is wanting and
      Living is dying.
And I say,
      "God, O God, See me before I pass,
      Tell me what is 'unity'
      Before my light is out and

I fade into history's dark corner.
Notice me on this mountain of time."

I fly to the sun and
    ride the falling stars and I know
I am a passing part of it all.

III

I waited patiently for the Lord;
he turned to me and heard my cry.
He lifted me out of the slimy pit,
out of the mud and mire;
he set my feet on a rock
and gave me a firm place to stand.
He put a new song in my mouth.
—Psalm 40:1–3 NIV

IV

It is a new song.
It is a praise song.
For Jesus came that I might know my God.

Redeeming the Page

I'm always torn whether to write my personal journal with a pen or a pencil. With a pencil, I can play with the page. I can erase, rewrite, and rearrange the words. I can work until the sentences flow in perfect cadence and rhythm. I can make it look perfect. But life is not perfect. I am not perfect. Most often when I journal, I want to leave out the stupid things I do or hurtful things I say. But we write our life in pen and ink. The reality of living is not written in pencil.

Our words and actions fall onto the day, in permanence. We can try to make changes, scratch out, amend, and insert afterthoughts around the edge of the page. But there is no editing of thoughtless actions or redoing of wrong or unwise choices. There is no eraser for hurtful words. When they are spoken, they are out there like a secret told. Our actions and words are written in ink. They simply are.

Often we feel guilty and hurt. How do we bridge the chasm created by disrupted relationships and harsh, angry words? Where do we find Hope? How do we get on balance again? How do we regain our sense of peace and wholeness? First, we return to the cross and ask forgiveness. We open ourselves to the Grace and Mercy God so freely gives. We say, "Here I am, Lord." Then we open ourselves to others. We accept personal responsibility and the risk of vulnerability. We begin to redeem the page by asking for and giving forgiveness.

Asking forgiveness is never easy. We always seem to stammer when the words "I'm sorry" or "please forgive me" are coming out. I remember one time when I was upset with a woman who I thought overcharged me for some services. I stewed for a while and then had a telephone conversation with her of which I am not proud. A while after our exchange of "words," I regretted what I said. I felt guilty; I felt awful. I felt off balance emotionally because my inner peace was fragmented. I needed to ask forgiveness. After I apologized and stammered out the "I'm sorry, please forgive me," I halfway thought she would say that she was sorry too. She did not. She just told me that she forgave me. I was a bit taken back. But inside me, where I live, I felt free and released. I had redeemed my page. I learned that day that asking forgiveness does not depend on the other person's response. It is an action I do regardless of the response. I also thought that I often stumble over such small stones.

Forgiveness is a gift. Have you ever needed forgiveness and received it; or given it to someone else when they needed it from you? If so, you have felt the release and the freedom forgiveness gives. It restores us. It allows us to begin again with ourselves and with another person. It redeems the page. Forgiveness is a gift that has its origin in God. God's plan of redemption and restoration of our relationship with Him begins at the cross. It means admitting we are guilty and asking for forgiveness.

The psalmist says, "If you, Lord, kept a record of sins, Lord, who could stand?" (Ps 130:3 NIV). Jesus forgives us. He redeems our page. He redeems our life.

Lord, thank you for Your forgiveness. Help me write my days with more care and more thought. Remind me to measure my words. Let me choose to be quick to listen, quick to forgive, slow to speak, and let my anger lag far behind.

Make My Words Simple and Clear

Lord,
Discipline my words with simplicity
Parse hidden meanings and subtitles
Subtract words that demand and words that wound
Razor-sharp words that speak too soon
Remove words on parade, words on ego's march
Side-mouthed words that gloat, words that are harsh
Words that pretend what I only half know
Words declared true, because I say so.
Parse my heart with integrity
Discipline my speech with simplicity.

The Opening

I

Our words stand between us like a wall
A self-defense against the intrusion of truth
Silence hangs heavy like a triple woolen coat.
Change is uncomfortable like ill-fitting clothes . . .
  either too small or too large to fit
Caring is sacrifice.

We spoke in selfishness and
Guarded the status quo.
So our words stand between us like a wall,
  a self-defense against the intrusion of truth.

II

Have we built so strong a wall
There is no breach, no hope of breaking through?
If so, this defender of the wall surrenders
   to caring and change and truth.
No wall should be without a gate.

III

Real wisdom, God's wisdom . . .
is characterized by getting along with others.
It is gentle and reasonable, overflowing with mercy
and blessings. . . . Do the hard work
of getting along with each another,
treating each other with dignity and honor.
—*James 3:17–18 The Message*™

Reminder Gifts

> . . . What is seen is temporary, but
> what is unseen is eternal.
> —*2 Corinthians 4:18 NIV*

Stepping back, the surgeon eyes his work and smiles.
Wrinkles stretched and snipped
He calls his labor "good, almost perfect."
Perhaps it was the nose (imperfect, left
Untouched by willful choice)
That made the face "almost."

The surgeon's tool of hand and eye
Sculpts the dust of clay and bones and
Slows the slant of summer sun,
But not even "almost" can he erase
The mysteries that weather the finite soul,

Not even almost, can he draw a line or angle to
Give beauty to the art of living. Not even almost, can
He remove, obliterate the birthmark
    the permanence of that ever-present, ever-
    deepening flatline.

These lines, these meant-to-be lines, cannot be
    smoothed.
They are Adam-etched, Ancient of Day lines: humble
    reminders of
Imperfections and willful choice,
Of short angled reprieves and tethered limitations;
Wrinkles of soul and sinew,
Reminder Gifts.

Mother: To Everything
There Is a Season

We expect our parents to die someday, but we are not ready for them to get old, to decline, to lose their strength and vigor, to have things wear out and go wrong with their body and . . . sometimes their mind. My family mourned the loss of our mother before it was time, before she actually died. But somewhere hanging over our head and always forged in our heart was the admonition "Honor your father and your mother" (Ex 20:12 NASB). In a long and lingering illness, sorrow comes early, and faith, grace, patience, and mercy must be our caretakers.

When my mother was seventy-three, she began a slow decline into mental illness. It was not dementia or Alzheimer's or even classic depression, although she was severely depressed. We finally concluded that it was something called Executive Function Disorder in which the brain is not able to prioritize incoming messages. The disease lasted ten years until she died at age eighty-three. It was a creeping downhill journey, so it was not until the last couple of years of her life that my mother, Louise, withdrew almost permanently into an old melon-colored recliner in her Phoenix, Arizona, sunroom. For many years, she would say, "God is God and I am not," or, "Maybe tomorrow will be better." And she did have some better tomorrows and we did have some good times together, but they got fewer and fewer until finally her only activity was the journey from the bedroom to the recliner. Although it stretches endurance, it is honoring to travel the "long road home" with an ageing parent. There are bittersweet, treasured memories along the way.

I remember one of our conversations on the telephone. After we had talked for a while, I said to her, "Mother, how does adversity affect one's character?" Without missing a beat, my seventy-nine-year-old mother said, "Margaret, it makes you strong, strong inside, and God comforts you." My dear mother who had been in a prison as real as any prison said adversity makes you strong and God comforts you. "Yeah, Mom," I said, "it does make you strong, but you know how we hate to exercise." If she smiled, I did not know. I suddenly wanted to reach out and touch her, wrap my arms around this woman and tell her how strong she was. I wanted to tell her that in her weakness she was adding to my faith.

During Mother's illness, I often flew to Phoenix. Each trip I thought, *This will be the last time that I see Mom alive.* The unraveling thread between her and the world was thin and frayed, like someone or something was pulling at the fabric. Even our talks on the telephone seemed to wear her out.

I remember one visit in particular. It was the time that I let go. I walked into the house and she was curled up in the recliner, looking like a small spring coil. She had been waiting for me. I walked over, bent down, and kissed her thin wrinkled face. "Thanks for coming, honey. I'm glad to see you one more time." She held up her boney index finger to indicate "one more." She had been dying for so long—death occupied, death fixated, death obsessed. Her body registered its betrayal. It seemed each day had squeezed the last remnants of life from her, like a flat, almost-empty tube of toothpaste. The illness and age seemed to have removed any gender softness. The boney angle of her body protruded in orthopedic landmarks. It was late and I went to bed.

That night, I woke several miles past midnight and my mind turned to the ins and outs of my visits home. I realized that I never seemed to make it without a frustrating dialogue. I would find myself wanting to shake her and say, "Behave yourself—think straight, be happy." I wanted her to be her old strong, critical, argumentative, and thinking self. But alas, she did not have enough energy to disagree or be disagreeable. She only had the horrible weight of despair.

In my midnight thinking I came to a conclusion: I needed to let go—let go of my need to control or change her, or even think I could make her better. I needed to accept Mother where she was and love her exactly the way she was. I needed to dispel my ignorance and arrogance in judging her. This was, to me, a great gift of grace, the freedom to open my hands and let go.

The next morning I awoke to the dull hum of the fan. A big clock read five till six. On the wall was a picture of Jesus, hands outstretched, rising from the clouds. Wrapped around the bedpost was a strip of leather made into a necklace that was strung with yellow, white, and blue beads with a rustic wooden cross in the center. At the door was Mother, closer to entering than lingering. She said, "Good morning, honey." I patted the bed and said, "Get in, Mom." She snuggled in the crook of my arms and we talked. I told her some of the things she gave to us girls. She taught all three of us sisters that fear was not in our vocabulary. She taught us to hold our heads high and our hearts humble. She encouraged us and told us we were special and we could do things if we just tried. She taught us how to cook and how to sew and how to be content with what we had. After a while, there was a pause. She knew I wanted her to be different, the same as she used to be, normal. Finally, she said, "You don't understand, Margaret." I looked over at her and said, "I know, Mom." I thought of the old hymn, "The things of earth will grow strangely dim, in the light of His glory and grace." I let go.

When do we know when to let go and rest in the rhythms of life, the abundance of God's Grace and the arms of His sovereignty? I think He tells us. And then He gives us peace.

Therefore we do not lose heart. Though outwardly we are wasting away, yet inwardly we are being renewed day by day. For our light and momentary troubles are achieving for us an eternal glory that far outweighs them all. So we fix our eyes not on what is seen, but on what is unseen, since what is seen is temporary, but what is unseen is eternal.
—2 Corinthians 4:16–18 NIV

The Choice

I

There are times when we want to take our mind on vacation. We want to escape the frenzy and just sit on a log in the still and quiet. There are times when we are pulled in many directions and pushed into other people's expectations. We want to take a break. There are times when multiple distractions or unexpected troubles weigh us down; there are times we search for answers.

When we get overwhelmed, there is hope and help and strength; the God whose eye is on the sparrow also cares about the challenges of our everyday lives. But it serves us well to know that one of God's greatest gifts to us is the ability to decide how we respond to life. We get to choose. We can roll over or we can get up and walk into the challenge. God is good and God loves us.

Margaret Wills

II

I would like to roll myself up in a tiny little ball
And fold myself over until there is no me at all.
I would like to fly to a place called Nowhere
A nice little corner without a cloud or a care.
However . . .
I fear I am wishing too much
Fantasies are just a fanciful crutch.
They are no help at all when I step back to earth
When my feet touch the ground and
   realities give birth.
So I will roll myself back, unfold my mind and
   unpack myself; there are answers to find.
Though my mind would like to rest and retreat
The Will of my spirit chooses to cast out defeat.
The God of my soul supplies each need.
There are things to do, there are challenges to meet.

III

For I can do everything God asks me
to with the help of Christ who gives me
the strength and power.
—Philippians 4:13 TLB

Talking Back

I

Every thought is a seed that reproduces itself. Negative thoughts, especially negative self-talk, produce more negative self-talk. Proverbs 4:23 says, "Above all else, guard your heart, for everything you do flows from it" (NIV). If the source of our thinking is negative, than that which flows from our conversation and behavior will be negative. Do we guard the way we talk to ourselves; or do we fill our mind with talk that is untrue, unproductive, and self-defeating? Do we keep pushing the "replay" button on negative thoughts in our head, thoughts that trap us in the past or cause us to fret about the future, thoughts that demean our ability to think for ourselves or act in a way that would produce change? We need to edit our negative self-talk, pause, and push the "erase" button.

Then we need to conform our thoughts to God's Word
and to God's view of our potential in Him.

II

I'm down today; my mind is on the ground today
   crawling around in the past.
It is meeting my memories and greeting my failures
   and laughing at my efforts of trying.
I'm down today; my mind is on the ground today
Embracing shattered dreams and broken possibilities.

Enough!

Memories are lessons for tomorrow.
They are fragments of a grand mosaic.
All that is broken becomes potential
When put into perspective.

So . . .
When my mind talks to me, I'll listen.
But when its talk dispirits me or
when it laughs at me for trying,
I'll pick it up and talk to it
And tell it to behave.

III

No, dear brothers, I am still not all
I should be but I am bringing all my
energies to bear on this one thing:
Forgetting the past and looking forward
to what lies ahead.
—*Philippians 3:13 TLB*

Come and Dine

I

God created the heavens and the earth and all that has life; He did not wave a magic wand but spoke everything into existence. He said, "Let there be light" (Gen 1:3 NIV). He created everything with His words. His words are permeated with life. The Word of God is life giving. Jesus said, "I am the bread of life" (Jn 6:35 NIV) and "I am the light of the world" (Jn 8:12 NIV). When we read or meditate on the scripture, we are coming to partake of spiritual life. The Bible is not just to be read. Its words are to be mulled over, chewed, and digested into our spiritual being much like food is assimilated into our cells to nourish us and give us physical life. Jeremiah 15:16 says, "Your words were found and I ate them" (NIV). Is your soul rushed and weary? Do you need the Bread of Life? Come to the table. Come and have a slow meal. "Taste and see that the Lord is good; blessed is the man who takes refuge in him" (Ps 34:8 NIV).

II

When your words came I ate them;
they were my joy and my heart's delight.
—Jeremiah 15:16 NIV

III

Come and dine. Let me take the time
To come and dine.
"It's not convenient, Lord,
I've got a lot of things to do.
Much for You,
Lord," my soul will say.
But I hear Your Spirit whisper, "Come and pray."
You know I need to be renewed
In the frustration of my rush,
So You bid my mind to hush and
My spirit to come and pray.
Come and dine. Let me take the time
To come and dine.
Fill the spirit part of me and
Slow down my busy mind
I will make the choice and take the time
To come to You and dine.

"Praise the Lord":
Passing on a Legacy

I

Several years ago, I was asked to speak on the topic "What Daughters Wished Their Fathers Knew." In preparing for the talk, I started thinking about my father. I concluded that it's the little things that a daughter remembers about her father—but they do remember. My father was as gentle as a summer soft breeze. When I was about eleven years old, I would go barefoot to my girlfriend's house that was about a block away. On occasion, I would stub my toe on the pavement. I would run home to cry. When I'd get there, Daddy would hoist me up on the kitchen counter and say in a slow voice, "Dog . . . gone . . . it . . . Margaret. That sure does hurt." I would stop crying, and he would wash it off and put some ointment and a Band-Aid on it. I'd hop down and hobble off. He said the same thing every time I hurt myself. I always felt better.

Now that my father is gone, what I wish my father knew the most was that his "Praise the Lord" exclamations still ring in my ears. It was a little thing but it was part of his character legacy to all of his children. This was especially true as he got older: I would get a good grade on a paper in graduate school, he'd say, "Praise the Lord." I would barely remember to put the salt in the meatloaf, he'd say, "Praise the Lord." I would call home to tell him I had passed a kidney stone I had been harboring for two months, he'd say, "Praise the Lord." It was a legacy of a little thing, but the words still stay in my ears. And I think they carried him into a thin place once shortly before he died but I'll never know for sure because it was just him and God doing business.

II

One fall, as Thanksgiving leaned into Christmas, I visited Daddy and Mother in Phoenix. I grew up in Phoenix, and it was to the Valley of the Sun I returned to stand in the lengthening shadows of my parents' lives.

One evening while my sister Betsy and I were in the sunroom, Daddy walked in with a cup of coffee.

He had on his blue plaid, flannel pajamas. Over them, he wore a neatly tied maroon bathrobe that one of us kids bought him a million years ago.

I remember telling my friends, when I was eleven or twelve, how handsome my daddy was. As he came into the room, I glanced up and smiled at my seventy-nine-year-old dad, who still had a touch of good looks left. Mother, who had been fighting some strange and insidious anxiety and depression, was curled up in her peach-colored recliner. There seemed to be only a breath of a woman left. Mom was tired. Dad was tired. He walked to his recliner and sat down and we began to talk.

There was a short pause in the conversion. Daddy took a deep breath, cleared his throat, and said, "I'm going to tell you a story I've never told before. One Christmas, when I was a little boy in Black Rock, Arkansas, I walked to the Baptist church at the top of the hill. There was a Christmas Eve service, and all the children were supposed to get a present. I didn't know that the presents had been placed under the tree secretly by the mothers of the children. You know, girls, my mother was just a child when I was born, only fifteen. Dad was eleven years older. He always loved Mother, but when she'd get mad, she would take off. That year, she was gone, taken off somewhere with my two little brothers. Well, anyway, there wasn't

Margaret Wills

any present for me under the tree, and I walked home, crying all the way."

"How old were you Daddy?" asked Betsy. "About twelve," he said. Daddy's thin lower lip quivered. He cleared his throat again and got up for another cup of coffee. Betsy and I looked at each other with tears. I leaned back and took a deep breath; I did not want to let go and cry like a little girl. I knew I'd be crying about too many things: the missing gift, the missing stories, the eroding edges of my parents' lives, the change and the continuity of life itself. I'd also be crying in gratitude. This common, blue-collar worker, but uncommon man, had fathered a family and given to his children a legacy of integrity, commitment, and faith. The moment could not handle my tears.

But the tears flowed later. I sat down and wrote a Christmas letter to Daddy. It was then that the tears that started with the story of the missing gift came.

Daddy,

When I was in Phoenix visiting you, you sat in your chair and told a "never-told-before story." It was about a little boy who cried all the way home from church because there was no present for him under the tree. For whatever reason, it failed to get there that Christmas. Your Father heard your sad cry and walked with you all the way home. You did not see Him or feel Him or know that He was there.

164

Over the years, He's given you gifts a thousand times more valuable than any you could find under any earthly tree. Your wife adores you. Your son and your daughters respect and honor you. They are indebted to you for the spiritual covering of prayers you provide for them, especially in the past several years. In your hardship, you have prayed for us all the more.

Don't ever quit saying "Praise the Lord," even in the small things like finding your car keys when you thought you lost them, or getting that first whiff of your bread rising in the oven. "Praise the Lord" is our heritage and your legacy.

You have lived the life of a good man who loved his family, who was loyal to his commitments. You were and are a faithful steward of all your gifts. So in this box, there is a gift: a model 1932 Ford Hi-Roadster, red of course, the color of boys' toys. It is for the little boy who cried all the way home one Christmas Eve a long time ago.

Keep it awhile and then give it to the "engineer," that great-grandson of yours who tears things apart and puts them back together again. Place it in his untested hand and tell him what you know. Tell him it was under the Christmas tree many years ago but you had to share your heart to receive it. Tell him it is OK to share your heart. And tell him God is still loving you and seeing you safely all the way home.

But along the way, there are still many reasons to say, "Praise the Lord."

And when you get home, bend your ear earthward and listen. Your children and their children will carry on, and join your song. "Praise the Lord" all the way home.

III

In 2006, I went to Phoenix for Christmas. During my stay, my daddy contracted a virus that resulted in a cough and a deep chest infection. His chronic lung disease did not give him any latitude when he got the slightest insult to his lungs. On Christmas day, we kids called 9-1-1 and the paramedics rushed him to the Emergency Room. When we got to the ER, it was packed with the elderly who, like Dad, had the flu. In fact, beds hugged the walls as many people waited for a hospital room. We waited for hours in a curtained off room. Finally, Daddy asked if he had a room yet. "No," my sister Shawn said with a smile, "beds are in short supply and there is no room in the inn." With a trace of a grin, Daddy said, "Well, I guess I'll just have to get in the manger." We all laughed as we always did at his quick, witty humor.

It took six hours before he was moved to a private room. He had a good first night. Again, with that quirky smile of his, he told me that he didn't know what they gave him last night but he wanted some more of it tonight. His humor was endless and enduring.

Shawn and I stood at the end of Daddy's bed and just looked at each other. We were dog-tired. "This," I said, "has not been a normal day." Normal days should be treasured. They make up the fabric of our life, and I think when hardship comes, what we long to do is return to the days when we just "lived life" before being interrupted by the unusual. We fail to savor the intimate nuances of everyday life and sift the gold of the sacred mundane.

On the third day, Daddy had a bad night. His breathing was labored. He slept deep for short periods of time and then he would open his eyes and be wide awake. When I arrived in the morning, he didn't respond to my presence. It seemed like a bit of his spirit was leaving. I thought he was fading. He asked several times if he was going to make it. Was it drugs or death I saw? I asked God for a good death if it came—a merciful peace to envelop him. Make his anxious worries go away. If this was the time, let him see Mother, smiling in the light with open arms, an embrace and a turning to walk hand-in-hand to the old porch swing in Arkansas, in the middle of a green, flower-drenched meadow.

He popped his eyes open and said, "Margaret, I love you." "I know. I love you too, Daddy." Daddy went back to sleep. I sat in the chair that was scrunched between the bed and the wall and began reading 2

Corinthians 4:18: "So we fix our eyes not on what is seen, but on what is unseen, since what is seen is temporary, but what is unseen is eternal" (NIV). It is strange we are to look at the unseen, look at something that our eyes cannot see. Francis Schaeffer says in his book *True Spirituality* that the greatest impediment to our experiencing true spirituality is that we fail to live the fact that there are two realities. Just like both halves of an orange makes the whole. We live our lives perceiving only one half of reality—the one we can see.

I flipped over to Colossians 1:15–16 where Paul says of Jesus, "The Son is the image of the invisible God, the firstborn over all creation. For in him all things were created; things in heaven and on earth, visible and invisible" (NIV). I thought, *So fix your eyes on what is unseen.*

When Daddy woke up, I told him the thought for the day was, "In him, all things hold together." We said it over and over again, and I began to realize that he was having more and more difficulty remembering and tracking. What I did not know at the time was that he was having small strokes that would erase a portion of his memory, especially his short-term memory. While we were saying our verse, a young girl came in with a mop and pail to clean the room. She said that she heard us reading the Bible. She then held up her wrist to show us what she had just proudly purchased in the gift store downstairs. It was a bracelet that said, "With him all things are possible." Daddy said, "Praise the Lord."

The young girl had tattoos all over her arms and ruby studs in her nose. God, how we judge a person by where we are coming from. Forgive me for the jillion times I do it.

Daddy drifted in and out of sleep. Each breath was a hard day's work. Each breath was a breathing rattle. Each breath was a breath closer to going or coming back.

When he woke up, he told me he saw Mother last night. I said, "Tell me about it." (Mother had died three years earlier.) He got an amused smile on his face and said, "You know, she was only this big." Then he gave the measure of the distance between his thumb and index finger. His smile gravitated into a chuckle, and he said, "I knew it was her because I recognized her thumb. You know, she used to use that thumb to scoop up the last bite of food on her plate." I knew the thumb he was talking about. How did he see the thumb when she was so small? Actually, she was about a year away. Daddy would see her the next Christmas.

I caught him smiling to himself, and I asked, "Daddy, what are you smiling about?" He said, "I was just thinking about when we were young."

His confusion walked in and out. He knew he couldn't figure it out, couldn't think straight. He asked many times, "What are we going to do?"

His sweet smile did not leave him. It was a smile of kindness, a smile like a soft breeze on a summer afternoon—it touched, but did not stay. What part of his mental landscape did it arise and to where did it retreat? His confusion and his smiles killed me.

Thank you, Lord, for the privileged moment of hanging on with him. Life, like joy, is momentary. Thank you for this honorable, loyal man. Let him see a glimpse of the invisible in order to remove all his fears for in You all things live and move and have their being.

When Daddy got out of the hospital, he could no longer live alone. My sister Shawn took him into her home where he lived for a year before he died. The day he came to her house, we took him into his room and got him settled. I was in the living room when I heard him. He was sitting in his wheel chair saying, "Praise the Lord," over and over again punctuated with "Praise the Lord, Bless His holy name." I peeked in and there he was with his hand raised in the air praising the Lord with all that was within him. I walked away and listened to him for about eight to ten minutes. I believe he was enveloped by the very near presence of God. Was he experiencing a thin place? I don't know but I believe so.

The night before he died, we children were all around. He said, "Where's Mother?" My brother Bill choked out, "She's gone to be with Jesus; don't you remember, Dad?" He smiled, looked up, and said, "We're family. We are all in this together." He never spoke again. He went to be with Jesus . . . and Mother. Praise the Lord. We begin as family and we end as family.

What do daughters remember about their father? It is the little things. Life is made up of the little things within the pleasures and challenges of our daily living. What character habits are we leaving our children and grandchildren as their spiritual legacy? Which ones do we want to intentionally cultivate? How about a spirit of praise which is born out of gratitude? Praise the Lord. Bless His holy name.

My Spirit's Song

I

When I see death—sullen and cold
I consider life's fragile hold
And I know that I will yield
To death's steady, silent stare
And lie still with folded hands
And eyes-closed empty glare.
I should be afraid with such a thought;
Except, by Christ's death I am bought
So, when I lie in earthly shroud,
Hear my Spirit sing aloud,
"Death cannot claim its victory
Because of Love at Calvary."

II

Since we, God's children, are human beings—made
of flesh and blood—he became flesh and blood too
by being born in human form; for only as a human
being could he die and in dying break the power of
the devil who had the power of death.

—Hebrews 2:14 TLB

"Death is swallowed up in victory."
O death . . . where then your sting?

—1 Corinthians 15:55 TLB

X

BEAUTY FROM ASHES

One Hundredfold:
To Steve and Judy in Memory
of Bethany Joy

I

It was shortly after seven on a Sunday morning when my friend Susan called me. "Margaret, Bethany Swift was killed in a car accident last night." I sucked in some air and thought, *O God, how can a parent's heart bear the weight of such grief?* Grief piled on grief. This was the third child Judy and Steve would bury: a stillborn baby, a toddler, and now a sweet college student, Bethany Joy.

The loss of a child is one of life's most difficult experiences. When one even thinks about it, the thought runs away in fear. Deep pain and severe darkness accompany the death of a child.

The next day, I went to Tulsa with four friends to visit the family. Little did we know that we would experience the paradox of the mingling of pain and

Grace as it filled the home when tens of dozens of friends came to express their sorrow. I watched Steve and Judy welcome their friends, cry, and stand in the middle of their Faith. But the thing I remember the most was Steve's words when I walked over to hug him. "What I'm working on," he said, "is not letting my thoughts get ahead of Grace." Since then, my mind has gone to those words a million times. Because I need to remember that God gives Grace in the present moment, not for the moments of our future.

Fear of the future paralyzes us, makes us scamper into the corner and wait—wait until we think it is safe. Job says that the days of our life are few and full of trouble. The apostle Paul says, "We are hard pressed on every side, but not crushed; perplexed but not in despair; persecuted, but not abandoned; struck down but not destroyed" (2 Cor. 4:8–9 NIV). When our path is dark and we think we cannot see the way, God provides the comfort of the Holy Spirit, the power of His Grace, and the light and guidance of His Word. Steve was right. We should not rush ahead of the One who promises to walk with us in the arid flatlands of fear and sorrow.

I saw Steve and Judy recently. I sensed that their Faith had served them well. They were proof that Grace sustains. They had not run ahead. They stood in the Grace of the moment. I asked them if I could

print the poem I had written to them in the dark days.
Steve beamed with a smile as big as his heart. He said,
"We would be honored."

II

But the seed falling on good soil refers to
someone who hears the word and understands it.
This is the one who produces a crop, yielding a
hundred, sixty or thirty times what was sown.
—*Matthew 13:23 NIV*

III

They roll over, together, with eyes open
Awake, but not really
They are somewhere in between the day and the dream
The "quiet" has begun.
They want to fall into the quiet;
But not really.
So they will rise, knowing
there will be another morning,
A next time and a next time
When some predicted something
or unpredicted surprise
Will shake the space that Joy filled
And they will remember a thousand things.

How does one unravel an hour or a moment,
And then reweave the fabric to make the day a
different shape?
How does the tapestry say to the Weaver
"I will not have that curve, that shape, that dark
umber of deep earth?"

It would have been easier if
Joy were not so . . . so abounding
So full, so overflowing, so "simply alive."
But then . . . the gift would have been less
And we also.

So they rise and together walk out of the "quiet."
Into the day, the day, the days.
Each day with its own Grace
The dross of grief will slowly fall and separate
But find no burial place. The heart is too deep.

But Joy, sweet Bethany Joy, goes on and on and on
In not one but many:
The harvest of one hundredfold.

Beauty from Ashes

I

It is to the prodigals . . . that the memory
Of their Father's house comes back.
—*Simone Weil*

In Luke 15, Jesus tells the story of a father who had two sons. The younger son asked for his part of the family estate as an early inheritance. After receiving it, the son left home, went to a foreign country, and wasted his fortune on wild and reckless living. He depleted his resources and a famine came over the land. He was alone. All he had was himself. He had to get a job. He found work in a pigpen, feeding pigs. One day, he was at the end of his rope and in despair: he was in a foreign country, he was abandoned by everyone, he had squandered his inheritance, and he had lost his relationship with his father. He was covered in naked shame. What he did not know was that he had not lost his father's love. He reasoned that his only hope was his father's mercy.

He headed home from the foreign country. And from far away, he saw his father running to him with open arms. The father embraced his son and kissed him. The son asked for forgiveness and mercy and then he heard his father say to his servants, "Quick, bring the best robe, put rings on his hand and shoes on his feet. Get a fattened calf. Let's celebrate. My son was lost and now he is found." Such is the Father's love.

Do you need to return home? The Father calls from the heavens and over the miles. When we are wayward, there is a way. Turn around, turn around; don't you hear the sound of love, calling, always calling? Love has a voice and Love has a name. "I will return to my Father's house." The return is always to the beauty of forgiveness and restoration.

II

When I look back at sin and separation,
At broken dreams and lonely desperation,
I am overcome with all that has been done.

But my Lord says to me,
"I'll give you beauty, beauty for ashes.
All that has been burned, I'll turn to beauty."
He says, "I will restore the years
That the locusts have eaten,
Your past is forgiven and I am making
Beauty for ashes."

When I think back, Lord, before I knew You
To time that used to be,
I want to undo things I've done
And cover all the harm.
But a day is lived and then it's gone
And many days I've lost—
So with Your Grace, I'll place them beneath the cross
As I hear You say to me,
"I'll give you beauty for ashes."

III

To bestow upon them a
crown of beauty instead of ashes.
—*Isaiah 61:3 NIV*

I will repay you for the years
the locusts have eaten.
—*Joel 2:25 NIV*

XI

REBIRTH

Hope

I

The snow melts as spring sighs.
Nature's green beauty waits
   to emerge from its winter embryo.
I wait—
For the sweet breath of spring
   and the surge of buds upon the trees,
       for new life and new growth.

But while the winter lingers,
   until it must give into the seasons,
I will savor its brown beauty and misty-grey cold
And although the brown and barren
   seem to speak of death,
Things are not always as they seem
And winter always yields to spring.

II

Be strong and take heart, all you
who hope in the Lord.
—*Psalm 31:24 NIV*

After the Storm: A Rainbow on Lake Champlain

I

You smile
When the sun breaks through
And I look up and point
And point again
   to Your Rainbow on a purple-slated sky.
In the storm, I have "a forgetting"
And then I see Your Promise:
A prism-arched picture:
A cathedral anchored on solid ground—
A psalm ascending, piercing the sky
A descending of heaven to earth
A reaching from earth to heaven
A promise seen after the storm.

II

It was an unusually hot summer in Burlington, Vermont. I sat on the porch of a little restaurant when the storm rolled in on Lake Champlain. Long fingers of lightning pierced the sky and then the sound of thunder tumbled over the water. It was a hard, quick rain, and about the time dessert came, it was over. As I sat eating the cheesecake I should not have had, I saw it. I got up, went over to the rail, and marveled at the almost-bright, ground-to-sky rainbow.

God is a giving God. A rainbow, like forgiveness, is a gift. It is given by God to remind us that He is a deliverer and a promise keeper. The biblical story of Noah and the ark (found in Genesis 6–9) points us to the first rainbow, the rainbow of promise. Evil had penetrated society so profoundly that God told Noah he planned to destroy the earth by water. Noah, in obedience to God, built an ark. He took his family and the animals into the safety of it. It began to rain, and it rained for forty days and forty nights. The incessant rain covered the face of the earth. Not even the nose of a mountain was exposed. It was a little over a year before Noah could walk on dry ground again.

Noah and his family were safe, but I imagine for Noah it was a wilderness experience. He must have grieved for all that was lost: his friends, his possessions, the ease of the familiar, the security of the predictable.

He was restricted to an enclosed area, a confined area with no sun and minimal light. There might have been family squabbles. Even the best of families have their moments. The smell from the animals had to be unpleasant, if not horrific. And then there was the waiting—the waiting for the rains to cease, for the storm to pass, and the sun to come out. There was the wait for deliverance. Noah had faith in the Lord, but I have to believe he was in a water wilderness. He didn't know when it would all end. He was ready to be on dry land.

We all have wilderness times in our lives when circumstances beyond our control confine us. Sometimes depression can take us out of the sun and we live with minimal light. Sometimes we have to endure unpleasant situations at work or conflicts within the family. There are the times when the rain keeps coming and coming and we want our feet on dry land. And then there is the waiting for the storm to pass, for things to be "normal" again. But like Noah, we continue not with despair but with faith in God because He is a God of promises. He is a God of deliverance.

When Noah finally placed his feet on dry ground, God had a conversation with him. He promised Noah that never again would He destroy the earth with water. And then He gave him a sign of that promise:

a rainbow. We worship a faithful God who delivers us and tells us to remember that His promises will not be broken. Are you standing on a promise of God? He is a promise keeper. Such is the message of a rainbow.

Blessed Are Those Who Have Not Seen Yet Believe—Part II

I

Give ear to my words, O Lord,
Consider my meditation.
—Psalm 5:1 KJV

II

Eternal Father,

I bow. My eyes cannot see You.
My mind cannot grasp Your Being,
Or Your power, or your eternal existence.
Your ways are beyond my brittle understanding.

Yet . . . it is Your Presence that quickens me,
Pulling my mind, my spirit, my existence toward You.

The goods and joys of this life are too small to satisfy.
My hunger and my thirst incline after eternal bread
and living water.

I thank you Father that You have not left me to
myself, alienated and adrift,
But You stand at the door and seek entrance.
Your presence illuminates my passage
And gives me knowledge of my eternal self.
I dwell in the unity of this knowledge and
The well-worn path of the known Way.

Let me not obscure Your Holy Light
From the lives of those who walk with me or see me
as I pass by.
Rather, let their vision be clarified by Your Holy
Spirit in me.

Today, as I bow before You and stand before a
watching world,
Let me go forth to enjoy this life with joy and
rejoicing, savoring each moment as a moment of a
meal, set before me, removed at day's end never to
be offered again.

My eyes cannot see. My mind cannot comprehend a
God such as You,

But You reveal to me essence and reality, both seen
and unseen.
And Your Spirit stirs in my heart
Satisfying eternal hunger, revealing eternal purpose
and confirming
That the Almighty God is also my
Eternal Father.

XII

AMEN

The Grand Plan

The story of the Gospel is love. The main theme of the Gospel is relationship. God wants us to know that He loves us. He wants us to respond to His revelation: the revelation of Himself in the person of Jesus Christ, the revelation of Himself as found in the Holy Scriptures, the revelation of Himself found in the communication of the Holy Spirit, and the revelation of Himself found in nature and the created order.

We receive revelation and come to relationship through God's Mercy and Grace and in our response to God through Faith. Our faith is not just a leap of faith; it is confirmed in redeemed reason. It makes sense that things are not the way they should be, that something terrible has gone wrong with the world and there should be hope, some way to fix it.

The answer lies in the Gospel. The story of the Gospel is summed up in five words: creation, death, redemption, restoration, and transformation. God created everything that exists in the heavens and on earth. We were created for God's glory and fellowship with Him. Our glory and purpose originates in relationship with God. In the Garden of Eden, man sinned and rejected God's authority and goodness. In one moment of time, all of creation fell from perfection; Satan slithered into the Garden in the form of a serpent. Man fell to the surety of evil, sin, suffering, and the sting of death.

God's love continued to reach out through His plan of redemption. He sent His Son, Jesus, to die on the cross for the forgiveness of our sins. Through faith, we are restored to our rightful relationship with God. When Christ rose from the grave and ascended to His Father, He sent the Holy Spirit to teach us and to comfort us and to change us. This comes through the process of ongoing spiritual transformation. Thus, we return to the glory of relationship to our Father, the God of the universe. This is the plan of salvation and the story of the Gospel.

Down through the ages, individuals have bowed their knee to the truth and the power and consolation of the scripture of John 3:16: "For God so loved the world that he gave his one and only son, that whoever believes in him shall not perish but have eternal life" (NIV).

Throughout history individuals have prayed the Sinner's Prayer:

Dear Lord, I admit that I am a sinner, and I confess my sins and believe that Jesus is the Son of God and He died for me and through faith in His death, burial, and bodily resurrection I am forgiven and have reestablished my relationship with You, my Heavenly Father, my Lord and my Redeemer.

Transformation

Jesus encourages us to see our short space of time on this earth in the light of eternity. He instructs us to remember that there are two realities: a physical reality and a spiritual reality. We are first and foremost spiritual beings called to follow Christ's teachings.

Jesus says we can trust our Heavenly Father. We are safe, we are protected, and we are guided when we cooperate with God's purpose and God's way of doing things. We become participants in the Kingdom of God and the Kingdom of God's Grace on earth.

Jesus reminds us over and over again that we must have Faith. We must believe in the fact that we are safe and that "good" will result as we submit our will to His Way. This submission is powerful. It defragments our life and gives us spiritual significance and wholeness of soul. This submission results in the process of spiritual transformation. Along the way, we are rewarded by "faith surprises" as resources of the Kingdom of Heaven are available to make changes in us, in others, and in the way things are.

Spiritual transformation is death to self. Everything in us wants to go kicking and screaming and talking about our rights and how right we are in any given situation. Fear wants to rise and speak to the bottom corners of our mind. It will remind us not to be vulnerable. We will remember what happens when we risk psychological safety or abandon feelings of superiority. We will remember our nakedness. We will feel the wash of old fears and the pull of old attitudes and the temptations of old behaviors. But our heart, where our choice and our spirit live, desires our Father and His Kingdom. And our Teacher taught us to pray.

When You Pray, Pray Our Father Your Kingdom Come

Our Father, who is in heaven, Holy is Your name.
Let Your Kingdom be established in us so that
What You are doing in heaven, we will see
   and hear and do on earth.
Give us this moment, this day.
Give us the Bread to sustain both body and soul.
Forgive us when we think and act against You
As we forgive those who think and act against us.
Forgive us when we trespass into Satan's territory.
Forgive us when we ignore Your desire
   and your power to deliver us.
You do not lead us into temptation.
No, You are the One who delivers us from evil.
You are the One who gives us power
   over Adam's ancient inclination.

Margaret Wills

You are the One whose Kingdom reigns
    in the Power and the Glory
Forever and ever,
    Amen and amen.
—inspired by Matthew 6:9–13

About the Author

Dr. Margaret Harrell Wills is dedicated to the ministry of encouragement, helping people experience hope, wisdom, and faith in their spiritual journey. Dr. Wills received her doctoral degree in higher education with a teaching field of history from the University of Arkansas. She taught history at the University of Arkansas in Fort Smith, Arkansas.

She is a writer and poet. She is a graduate of Chuck Colson's Centurion Program for Worldview Leadership. Her home is in the foothills of the Ozark Mountains in Fort Smith, Arkansas, where she lives with her husband, Paul.